The
Stigma
of
Calvary

The Stigma of Calvary

by
Lester Sumrall

LeSEA Publishing Co.
P.O. Box 12
South Bend, IN 46624

THE STIGMA OF CALVARY

Copyright © by Lester Sumrall Evangelistic Association, Inc.

2nd printing
Published by LeSEA Publishing Company
P.O. Box 12, South Bend, Indiana 46624

Printed in the United States of America.
All Scripture quotations are from the King James Version of the Bible.

ISBN 0-8407-5720-4

Contents

The Stigma of Calvary

Introduction

Holy Communion is essential to the spiritual life of Christians. It is not optional. We are commanded by our Master to receive it. It is no more optional than water baptism. We are told to be baptized in water. Romans 6 says those who are buried with Christ in baptism shall rise with Him in resurrection. Likewise the Scripture says, "For as often as ye eat this bread, and drink this cup, ye do shew the Lord's death till he come" (1 Cor. 11:26). In receiving the Lord's Supper we are carrying out the command of our Lord and Master.

There have been many discussions regarding Holy Communion. This is sad, for I feel that simply *receiving* Communion is the most important thing. Once I preached for a church in Ireland. I ministered to them for an entire week. On Sunday morning I was the one who preached; but when they took Holy Communion, they told *me* to sit in a corner. I could not receive it with them because I did not belong to that local body.

"But I have preached to you all week," I said. "The people have loved my preaching and my teaching. Many people have been won to the Lord for your church this week."

But they answered, "We are sorry. You cannot receive Holy Communion with us because you do not belong to our church." Because my name was not on their membership rolls I could not receive the Lord's Supper. I believe that attitude would grieve the Lord Jesus Christ. It shows how narrow-minded people can be regarding who shall receive Holy Communion.

The Lord's Supper does not belong to an individual church. It does not belong to Roman Catholics. It does not belong to Protestants. It is the *Lord's* Supper. When we look at it from this viewpoint we see it in proper perspective.

When I was living in Hong Kong, pastoring a church called New Life Temple, there was a large Chinese church in Kowloon, across the harbor from us. It had two pastors.

On Sunday mornings one of the pastors would serve Communion. When he came to the bread he would say, "I will cut the bread. I will not break with my hands the holy body of the Lord Jesus Christ."

The other pastor would lead the evening service. When it came time to serve the bread, he would break it and say, "I want you to know we break the bread. I would not cut it, seeing it symbolizes the body of the Lord. I could not use a knife to cut the body of our Lord Jesus Christ."

The church divided itself because two ministers wondered if it were proper to cut the bread with a knife or to break it by hand. The Lord must have been very sad. Yet we frequently allow little things like that to hurt and injure many who belong to the Lord Jesus Christ.

I am glad to say that in our services all those who know they are washed in the blood of the Lord Jesus can participate in the Communion, regardless of their church affiliation. The way the bread was handled before distribution was not a matter of special significance.

What is Holy Communion? Most of us have participated in it at some time. Holy Communion is a memorial to the New Covenant, or New Testament, through which we enjoy a new relationship with the Lord Jesus Christ. He provided this new relationship through His death. Through Holy Communion we recall that Christ died for us and that we have salvation because of His death. He has left us emblems representing His body and His blood. The bread speaks to us of the body of our Lord, broken by the stripes that were inflicted on Him. The cup represents the blood shed by our Lord. It speaks to us of eternal salvation, of redemption through His precious blood.

We frequently hear the ordinance referred to as the Lord's Supper or the Lord's Table. These names stress that it is the Lord's and not the exclusive property of any one group or individual. At other times we may call it Holy Communion, because it is a time of communing in a personal, intimate way with our Lord Jesus. By any name, this ordinance is inexorably linked to the death of Christ. It points to the cross. It is a memorial to the One who died, yet is not dead. It points to the grave, yet is intended for those who have eternal victory over the grave.

The Lord's Supper is more than mere form or ritual. It is a source of healing, for it memorializes the stripes by which we are healed. It is a source of fellowship, for in observing it we come into fellowship with others who know Christ as Lord. It is a reminder of the constant union we enjoy with the Savior. The Lord's Supper is a grand paradox. It is a memorial to One who needs no memorial. It looks backward at death as a defeated foe, rather than forward to it as a dreaded villain. It points to a broken body and shed blood, yet views death as the beginning of life. The Lord's Supper speaks of death, yet its subject is life. Its bread is the bread of life, its cup the cup of life.

In these pages we hope to present Holy Communion in a light by which it is seldom illuminated. We hope to show that Communion is not a lifeless picture of events gone by, but a living link to eternal spiritual truth. We hope to illustrate that the Lord's Supper is a doorway into a deeper and richer communion with Christ than most believers realize. It is a memorial; but more than that, it is life.

1
The Feasts That Jesus Gave

"Then Jesus called his disciples unto him, and said, I have compassion on the multitude . . ." (Matt. 15:32).

Jesus had compassion on the multitude. Weymouth's translation of this passage says, "My heart yearns for this mass of people." Some people cannot see a crowd. They may be pushed by a crowd, jostled about by it, but never really see it. Jesus, on the other hand, had compassion on the crowd. He saw it not as a mass, but as individuals in need. Possibly the greatest need of the church in this age is to realize that there are over four billion human beings living in the world at this very moment. Jesus has compassion on each of them. His church must also. Jesus' words in the above passage were spoken just before His feeding of the four thousand. By His own choice, Jesus was poor in this world's goods. Yet in spite of His poverty, Jesus gave several feasts. We should consider three of these occasions.

CHRIST FEEDS THE MULTITUDES

The feeding of the four thousand, as presented in the above passage and verses that follow it, is a

13

miracle distinct from the feeding of the five thousand. Many think the two accounts refer to the same event, the number given in one account being a mistake. Such is not the case. Many distinct points separate the two feasts. Each was, however, an important milestone in the Lord's earthly ministry. Each marked the close of a portion of His ministry. This is a significant fact.

In Matthew 14 Jesus closed His ministry in Galilee with a feast. It was in Galilee that Jesus had spent His childhood and the greatest part of His ministry. The feast began with five barley loaves and two fishes given to Jesus by a small boy. Jesus took those loaves and transformed them. He multiplied them. He fed a multitude with them. The Scripture says Jesus fed five thousand men, not counting women and children. Only the Lord knows exactly how many were fed that day, but what a miracle it was! Imagine the joy the little boy must have experienced as he saw his meager lunch provide miraculous satisfaction for so many.

The second feast Jesus gave was for the heathen multitudes of the region of Decapolis. Decapolis ("ten cities") was an area across the Sea of Galilee from the site of the first feast. It was the region in which Jesus had cast the legions of devils out of the demon-possessed man. The people that Jesus fed in Matthew 15 were not Jewish people and were not the religious people among whom He had lived. They were heathen. On this occasion He took seven loaves and a few fishes and fed four thousand men, besides women and children. When the feast was over seven baskets of food were collected, not twelve, as at the earlier feast. At the first of these two feasts Jesus showed compassion for those among whom He had lived and walked. In the second He showed compassion for those who had heard so little of the gospel. The two occasions occured close in time as Jesus closed His ministry in those two areas.

CHRIST FEEDS HIS DISCIPLES

As Christ approached the final hours of His earthly life, He gave a third feast, perhaps the most significant of any in which He participated. He shared this feast with the inner circle of His disciples just before He died. It was a meal shared privately and lovingly with those who had walked with Him, who had known Him, who had loved Him much. Jesus knew His time with these disciples was drawing to a close. He wanted them to see that the special relationship between Him and the masses was an eternal one. He wanted to show them that the responsibility of spreading the Word of Life was soon to become theirs.

Just as the disciples had once walked through the seated crowds distributing baskets of miraculous food, so would they soon pass among the needy multitudes sharing the Bread of Life. Just as they had given bread and fish to the multitudes to satisfy their hunger, so would they soon give Jesus to the masses to satisfy their souls.

CHRIST'S DISCIPLES FEED THE WORLD

The church is in the same position today as Jesus' disciples were in the first century. We are to stand

15

between Him and the masses, the vast multitudes of humanity. We are the only ones who can transmit to the multitudes the compassion that Jesus feels for them. He pities them, and has an infinite empathy for them. We must become infused with the same feeling, the same love, the same mercy that our Lord Jesus Christ exhibited. We are the only medium through which His love and the love of heaven can flow to the millions on earth who have never heard the gospel. We must take the loaves that the Lord Himself has broken with His own tender touch and offer them to the crowds of unhelped and unhealed.

If the church, through Holy Communion, could again see Jesus broken and given to the multitudes to feed and care for them, we would be a new people. We would be a powerful people, victorious by His might. We would share the compassion that Jesus felt. We would realize anew that Jesus is as able to feed the multitudes and bring life to the millions as He was on the hillsides surrounding the Sea of Galilee. That drive which Christ had within Himself, He wishes to place within us. We are not sufficient within ourselves to feed the multitudes. Christ, however, is sufficient for every need of humanity.

Jesus told His disciples to seat the crowds and feed them, but the disciples had no food to offer. So Jesus took a small portion of bread, broke it, and miraculously provided enough for everyone. Jesus asks us to throw ourselves completely at His feet and confess that He alone can meet the need of the world.

There is none other like Him. No one else can offer the world the strength or help it needs. There is no hope outside of Jesus. The only hope for those billions who are without Christ is seeing His broken body and shed blood. They can only see Him through His church. This was true when Jesus met with His disciples in the upper room, and it is still true today. Just as the multitudes would have gone away hungry had the disciples not distributed food to them, so the people of the world today can never know life eternal unless the people of God present the message of Christ to them.

There is another dimension to the feeding of the five thousand, and later the four thousand, that deserves special attention. Jesus began with a small quantity. He broke the food and gave it to His disciples. Had they ceased at that point, or any later point, in giving food to the multitudes, the source of supply would have dried up. If they had quit when the job was half finished, the miracle would have ceased. As long as there were people to feed, there was a source of food.

This principle may help us understand one of the major problems facing the church in our generation. In many instances we have received the blessings of God and held them ourselves, but because we have not shared the message, it has ceased to be powerful or glorious; it has ceased to save the multitudes. Only as we share the message of Christ does the message become powerful. Only as we share it does it perform the miraculous. Only when we hand the broken body and shed blood to the perishing does an infinite supply flow into our hands.

The church needs to realize that in the Communion

of our Lord and Savior, there is a supply that cannot be measured. Every need of humanity can be met there. When the disciples gave food, there was more to give until everyone had been satisfied. When we give, it is given unto us again. God provides blessings pressed down, shaken together, and running over. When a believer gives, God gives more. When a church gives, God gives more. It is the principle of multiplication; we only receive as we give. If we do not give, we do not receive. The church, with its modern disciples of Jesus Christ, must be alert to the fact that the message of Communion with Christ cannot be hidden. Closed up, it will die.

The message that Jesus shared with His disciples in the final feast must be distributed as faithfully as the broken bread and fishes that were shared in the first two feasts. If we do not share the message, it will not live. If we do not give it to others, it cannot give life. The truth of the upper room, the truth of the third feast, the truth of Holy Communion, must be given to the multitudes just as it was given to us.

Jesus said, "Take, eat; this is my body. And he took the cup, and gave thanks, and gave it to them, saying, Drink ye all of it; For this is my blood of the new testament, which is shed for many for the remission of sins. But I say unto you, I will not drink henceforth of this fruit of the vine, until that day when I drink it new with you in my Father's kingdom" (Matt. 26:26-29). The first two feasts were prompted by Christ's compassion for the multitudes, but were followed by no particular promises. The final feast was also prompted by compassion for the multitudes but was

18

closed with the magnificent promise that Jesus would give not broken bread, but His own body and blood. Holy Communion is far more than mere religious form. It is a life-giving message to be shared with the masses. It is a message of healing and hope and union with Christ. It is a message of eternal life. In these pages we will explore that message and its meaning to those who believe and to those who are in need of salvation.

2
The Lord's Supper

As we have already noted, Holy Communion is more than mere ritual. The celebration of this ordinance places us in direct communication with Christ. It is the most beautiful of the practices of the Christian faith and can become the source of powerful spiritual blessings.

In the Scriptures we see two assemblies or churches. The first is described in the Old Testament: the nation of Israel. The second, in the New Testament, is the body of Christ. The Greek word most frequently translated "church" is *ecclesia*. It can mean "those who are called out." We who have trusted Christ are called-out ones. Both of God's assemblies were called out by miraculous deliverance. Israel was called out of Egypt and brought into the land of promise. The new body has been, and is being, called out of sin and death and brought into union with the Lord Jesus Christ. God celebrated a special feast with both of His assemblies. In the Old Testament there was the Passover. In the New Testament there is Holy Communion. Both are celebrated to help us remember the moment of deliverance.

THE NATURE OF THE SUPPER

Of what should we be reminded when we consider the Lord's Supper? First, we ought to remember that it is the *Lord's* Supper, not man's. Our Lord and Savior, Jesus Christ, initiated it; it was not born in the hearts of men. It was not instituted by church councils. It is not a ritual that has been added to the church. The Lord's Supper is an original function of the church, one that has been observed from the beginning of church life. Christ initiated it, and in so doing He became, in a remarkable and mysterious fashion, the very memorial we observe today. The Lord *is* the Lord's Supper.

We do not mean to say that the bread we partake of is literally and chemically transformed into the flesh of Jesus of Nazareth. We do not mean to imply that the fruit of the vine is literally and chemically transformed into His blood. However, we cannot overemphasize the truth that when we eat of the bread and drink of the cup we take unto ourselves the essence of Christ Himself.

What better way to picture such a transaction than by eating and drinking? Nutritionists have long told us that we become what we eat, or more accurately, what we eat becomes us. Today's muscle and bone were last week's meat and milk. Today's bread and fish will become next week's blood and tissue. The one who eats and the thing that is eaten eventually become one. Our union with Jesus Christ is the same. As we take Him, we become one with Him, and He one with us. It is communion, a common union or

22

bond between the Lord and the individual believer. It is the Lord coming to man. It is His supper, His table, His fellowship. It is not a church's supper, or a denomination's supper. It is *His* supper.

THE PARTAKERS OF THE SUPPER

To more fully understand the Lord's Supper we must not only see that it is His, but we must understand with whom He is pleased to share it.

To whom, indeed, was that first celebration of this ordinance presented? The first Communion of our Lord was given exclusively to His disciples, the apostles. It was not given to His enemies, that they might mock Him and sneer at Him. There was no place at that table for anyone who was not a disciple. You will remember that Judas left before Jesus passed the bread and wine. This fact shows us that Holy Communion is not for the unbeliever. The unregenerated man or woman has no place at the Lord's table. We have already seen that in partaking of this supper we celebrate and come into a personal and intimate relationship with Jesus. We are one with Him. This union is only possible because we have been born into His family through salvation.

As baptism shows, we have accepted His death as our death to sin, and as payment in full for sin's penalty. We have accepted His burial as the putting away of our old nature. We have accepted His resurrection as the coming to life, or quickening, in us of God's Spirit. We are dead to sin and alive to

God. That which we once were, a son of Adam, became totally unacceptable to God. However, in Christ, that old man was put away and a new man was born. Only that new man can come into union with Christ. Only that new man can know the intimacy of Holy Communion with the Lord of glory.

How can that which is totally unacceptable to God come into union with His Son? It cannot. Certainly, the bread may be eaten and the cup partaken from, but there can be no communion. Paul, writing by divine inspiration, gave stern warnings to those who would eat the bread of communion or drink from the cup unworthily. We will deal with those warnings more thoroughly in a later chapter. At present, it is enough that we understand that the Lord's Supper is offered exclusively to those who are the Lord's by new birth.

THE COMMUNION OF SAINTS

Our unity with Christ in Holy Communion should have a profound effect on our attitude toward other brothers and sisters in Christ. Let us turn to some simple mathematics to illustrate this truth. Imagine that we are dealing with three unknown quantities or numbers. We will use the letters A, B, and C to represent those numbers. With this in mind, consider the following equations:

$$A = B$$
$$A = C$$
$$B = C$$

If A is exactly equal to both B and C, then it follows

that B and C are equal. Look at the process again, this
time using numbers:

$$2 + 3 = 5$$
$$1 + 4 = 5$$
$$2 + 3 = 1 + 4$$

If we add the numbers two and three, we always get
five. If we add the numbers one and four, we always
get five as well. If two plus three equals five, and one
plus four equals five, then two plus three must be
equal to one plus four.

Our relationship to Christ and to other believers is
as graphic as the relationship of the various equations. Let us repeat the process a final time. Instead
of A, B, and C, let us use Christ, You, and Me. Note
the effect:

You are united with Christ.

I am united with Christ.

Therefore, you are united with me.

It is not a question of whether you are a member of a
certain church or denomination. It is not a question of
whether I am united with a certain church or denomination. The vital question is whether you and I are
united in Christ. If we are united in Christ, eating the
bread and drinking of the cup together at His table,
then all other distinctions dim by comparison.

Many would contend that you cannot take Communion with me, nor I with you, unless we both are
members of the same local church or denomination.
The church, they would say, is responsible for seeing
to it that no one partakes of the Lord's Supper
unworthily. I do not see this in Scripture. When, in 1
Corinthians 11, Paul pronounces penalties for those

who abuse the Lord's table, he pronounces those woes upon individuals, not upon the group. We see, then, that celebration of Holy Communion brings those who have trusted Christ into a personal and intimate fellowship and union with Him and with one another, regardless of church or denominational ties.

THE SIGNIFICANCE OF SYMBOLISM

As we understand the union with Christ and our fellow believers that is ours through the Lord's Supper, we come to a fuller appreciation of the symbolism of the elements and practices of the Lord's table. The cup of blessing represents the blood Jesus shed for us. He said of the cup, "This is the blood of the new testament, which is shed for many" (Matt. 26:28). As we look back into the Old Testament, we cannot escape the striking parallel between the Lord's Supper and the Passover Feast. In fact, it was at the observance of Passover that the Lord's Supper was instituted. The one pointed forward to the other. The Passover was a time of witness. The father of each household explained to his children how the death angel had passed through Egypt. In every home where the blood of the sacrificial lamb had not been applied to the door post, the first-born died. That sacrificial lamb was a symbol of Jesus Christ. That blood was a symbol of His blood. That deliverance from death was a picture of the deliverance that Jesus gives to all believers. The Passover was a witness to the gospel of Christ, even before Christ came.

Just before Jesus fulfilled the death that the Passover predicted, He instituted His new feast. That feast is also a witness. It is a witness to the broken body and shed blood of the Savior. It is a witness to the fact that only in Jesus is there hope of deliverance. The saints of Israel were to observe the Passover with regularity, each time explaining and reinforcing the message that deliverance and life could only come through the shed blood of the lamb. It was a major aspect of Jewish life. People talked about it and told others about it. They explained it to their children. All Israel knew and understood that on that dark day in Egypt, a lamb died so that a nation might live. The Passover constantly called that fact to their attention. Likewise, the Lord's Supper should be a constant witness to us that we can only have life through the death and resurrection of God's eternal Lamb. He died so that we might live.

We ought, therefore, to share that message. Just as the Jews told it over and over again, so should we talk about it, tell others about it, and share it with our children. The Lord's Supper should be a constant witness to us, and to others, of what we have received in Christ Jesus.

The Lord's Supper also teaches us of the enduring nature of Christ's work. Paul wrote: "For as often as ye eat this bread, and drink this cup, ye do shew the Lord's death till he come" (1 Cor. 11:26). Jesus Himself told the disciples that He would not drink the cup with them again until they drank it together in His kingdom. The disciples understood this to mean Christ's eternal kingdom. So should we.

The observance of the Lord's Supper is to continue

until Christ returns to earth to claim His church and establish His everlasting kingdom. This continued observance not only witnesses God's grace, but also shows us that God's grace will be continually active until the Lord's return. Jesus' broken body and shed blood will go on giving new life and new hope to men and women until the day that Christ Himself returns to earth. Then, as He promised His disciples, He will drink of His cup with us in that kingdom. The salvation represented by the Lord's Supper is as enduring as the drinking of the cup, and the drinking of the cup is to continue until the Lord's return, and then on into eternity. The Lord's Supper speaks to us, each time we observe it, of the eternal work Christ has done in us.

The ordinance also speaks of safety. If you were to ask an Israelite from those ancient days what the Passover meant to him, he might answer "safety." For ancient Jews, blood on the doorposts meant protection from death. All who were inside the house marked with the blood were safe. There is also an element of safety in the Lord's Supper. As we observe the ordinance, as we drink of the cup, we can rejoice in the knowledge that God will not judge us. He loves us. We are His own. When He sees the blood of Christ applied to the doorposts of our hearts, there is no judgment. The judgment for sin has already been carried out. When the death angel saw the blood, he knew that the lamb had died. The evidence of the lamb's death was smeared over the door. The blood seemed to cry out, "Pass over. Death has already come here."

The blood of Christ declares that judgment has already been executed. Herein is safety. Christ has borne our judgment. When we receive the elements of the Lord's Supper we can be reminded of the safety we enjoy in Christ. There is no reason to fear. We need not be afraid to live, for Christ lives in us and is able to deal with all circumstances that might confront us. There is no need to fear death, for Christ has already died on our behalf. In living we have safety, in dying we have safety. As often as we drink of the cup and eat the bread, we are reminded of our safe position in Christ.

We can enjoy that safety because God is satisfied. He is satisfied with the death, burial, and resurrection of Christ. The broken body and shed blood of Christ are enough. Nothing more is needed. Christ died to become the propitiation for our sins. He satisfied the demand placed upon us by God's righteousness. God is righteous. Man is unrighteous. It is impossible for God to allow the unrighteous to go unpunished. He cannot and will not allow the unrighteous to enter into His holy presence. How, then, can man hope to approach God? He cannot, until his sin and unrighteousness have been judged, not until God is satisfied that judgment has been executed.

God is not only righteous and just, but also loving. He loves us and wants to draw us to Himself. Still, the matter of unjudged sins must be dealt with. Therefore, God has provided His Son to satisfy the demands of righteousness, and the Son has satisfied those demands completely. We are now able to enter into God's presence without fear, knowing that God is satisfied with the payment for our sins. Christ is the payment, the propitiation, the satisfaction for all the penalties of unrighteousness. He is enough. No more is required. As we view the Lord's table the elements witness to us anew that Jesus is enough.

Jesus has become our propitiation. God is satisfied. It is not a matter of feeling; it is a matter of fact. The blood has been shed and applied to the doorpost. The demands have been met, and we have been redeemed. We have received a new life in Christ and a new power that we did not possess before. Our sins are gone, really gone! The blood declares it.

Because the Lord's Supper witnesses to our enduring safety in Christ, its celebration and observance should be a feast of praise. We have received something about which we can rejoice. It should be a time when we thank God that we are saved. We do not receive the Lord's Supper because we are members of a church. We receive the Lord's Supper because our sins have been washed away. This is not a matter of subjective opinion. It is a matter of objective truth. God has promised He will wash away the sins of those who trust His Son Jesus Christ. When we trust Christ, asking Him to forgive us of our sins, God washes our sins away. They are gone; knowing this, we can praise God.

One of the more interesting aspects of the blood of the Passover lamb was that it acted as a seal. The blood on the door sealed the house against intrusion by the angel of death. It was a "no trespassing" sign. Stay away, it declared, this house is sealed by God. The Bible tells us that if our sins have been washed away by Jesus' blood, then we are sealed by the Holy Spirit. He acts as a "no trespassing" sign against death, sickness, and Satan. The devil has no right to enter our lives once the Holy Spirit has sealed us unto God. When the devil brings things into our lives it is only because we have allowed him access. When we trust God, and by the power of God resist the devil, we are victorious.

Satan is powerless to cross the threshold of any heart sealed by the Holy Spirit. The Lord's Supper reminds us of this truth. It becomes grounds for rejoicing. Who can help but praise God at the realization that his sins have been washed away and that he has been sealed against harm from Satan through the Spirit of God?

THE SUFFICIENCY OF CHRIST

All that God gives us, has given us, and will give us, comes to us through Jesus Christ. It is all of Him, none of us. At the risk of belaboring the point, we must repeat that His role is giving; ours is receiving. He gives us the broken body. He gives us the shed blood. We do not take them on our own. We do not add to them, we receive them as He has given them. In the Passover, the Jews were required to do nothing other than apply the blood. They did not have to bar the door. They did not have to erect a fence. They merely applied the blood and believed that the blood was enough. It was. It still is.

God gives. We receive. God does. We believe. No more is required. We mention this again, not because

31

of its complexity, but because of its simplicity. It is too simple for some. Some would add requirements of duty to the grace of receiving. God does not. Others find it easy to receive in one area, but more difficult to receive in others.

We have spoken a great deal in this chapter of the blood. We have said little about the broken body. Yet the broken body of Christ, and the bread which represents it to us, are very important. When Jesus served the bread to His disciples, He broke it and told them it was His broken body. We know that not a single bone in Jesus' body was broken. This is the fulfillment of prophecy. The leg bones of the thieves crucified beside Jesus were broken, but none of Jesus' bones were broken. How, then, was His body broken? It was broken through the beating and abuse He suffered. The Roman scourge was used to lay stripes on His body. This is the breaking of which He spoke. The prophet Isaiah wrote: "But he was wounded for our transgressions, he was bruised for our iniquities: the chastisement of our peace was upon him; and with his stripes we are healed" (Isa. 53:5).

In 1 Peter 2:24 the apostle makes it clear that these prophetic words of Isaiah refer to Jesus by quoting them in reference to Christ. Note particularly that last phrase: ". . . by whose stripes ye are healed." We know that Jesus' shed blood washes away our sins. We accept that as truth. But do we realize that Jesus' broken body gives us healing? We believe that God has forgiven our sins. His Word declares it. Should we not also accept what the Word declares about our healing? All of our sins were borne by Jesus on Calvary. Their power over us has been broken. They have been put away forever. Likewise, Jesus has already borne on Calvary all our sickness and infirmity. They should, therefore, have no more power over us. When we receive the cup of blessing we rejoice that God has given us the forgiveness of sins. When we receive the broken bread, should we not also rejoice that God has already provided everything that is necessary for our healing?

We often overlook this aspect of Holy Communion, yet it is as valid as any other part of the ordinance. There are many who, if they fully understood the meaning of this ordinance, could feel the healing power of Christ in their own bodies while receiving the Lord's Supper. It is not that the bread contains magic power. It is only bread. However, when we receive that bread and view it as Christ's broken body, we realize that Jesus has provided our healing in Himself. At that moment our faith may be quickened and the door opened to God's restoring power.

When we come to the Lord's table, we should not be afraid to come there for healing. He has provided that healing already in Christ Jesus.

The broken bread speaks of healing of our physical bodies. The shed blood speaks of the washing away of our sins. God wishes for us to receive healing and to rejoice in His secure salvation. In the Lord's Supper He has given us a reminder of both these wishes.

We come together around His table, not because we are worthy, nor because we belong to the right church or denomination, nor because we hold any particular office within our local church. We come to the Lord's table because we have been born into His family. We celebrate the Lord's Supper as a means of entering into a personal and intimate communion and union with Him, and with our fellow believers. That supper is a reminder, or witness, to us of the enduring nature of God's work in us, of the safety we enjoy because of that work, of the complete saving and sealing that Jesus has accomplished on our behalf, and of the healing that is available to us through Him.

3
What Mean Ye by This Sacrifice?

We have seen that there is a parallel relationship between the Passover feast of the Old Testament and the Lord's Supper of the New Testament. Listen to the Old Testament's instructions concerning the Passover feast:

> And it shall come to pass, when your children shall say unto you, What mean ye by this service? That ye shall say, It is the sacrifice of the LORD's passover, who passed over the houses of the children of Israel in Egypt, when he smote the Egyptians, and delivered our houses. And the people bowed the head and worshipped (Exod. 12:26,27).

Compare those words to the instructions of the New Testament:

> This cup is the new testament in my blood: this do ye, as oft as ye drink it, in remembrance of me. For as often as ye eat this bread, and drink this cup, ye do shew the Lord's death till he come (1 Cor. 11:25,26).

These passages show us that both feasts were

intended to serve as memorials, reminders, signposts to direct us to spiritual truth. Because the Passover was established by the same God who established the Lord's Supper, and because it was intended to point to the truths the Lord's Supper symbolizes, we should not be surprised that we can learn much about one by studying the other. We cannot fully understand the Passover lamb until we are aware of Jesus as the great Lamb of God who gave Himself for the salvation of the world. By the same token there are some aspects of the Lord's Supper that can be better understood by a study of the Passover.

PASSOVER: ITS RELATIONSHIP TO COMMUNION

Let us consider the requirements for partaking of the Passover feast. The first requirement was circumcision. All males who would participate in the Passover were required to be circumcised. The rite of circumcision set Israel apart from other nations. It depicts, in a figurative sense, the cutting away of the old nature. Before a Jew could participate in the Passover, he had to submit to circumcision. Before being eligible to receive Holy Communion, one must have cut off those things that are of the world. We should do away with those things that are nonspiritual, things that would hinder us from entering into the holy presence of God.

The second thing the Jews had to remember was that no stranger was invited to eat the Passover feast. Those who were not of Israel could take no part in the Passover. For them it would be a memorial without meaning. Their fathers had not been imprisoned in Egypt. Their ancestors had not known the Pharaoh's bondage, nor the threat of the death angel, nor miraculous deliverance by the blood of the lamb. The entire ritual would have been meaningless to anyone not of Jewish heritage.

The same principle applies to the Lord's Supper. As we have already seen, there is no place at the Lord's table for the unregenerated. The unconverted must not be asked, or invited, or permitted to receive the Holy Communion. It would be as meaningless to them as the Passover would be to someone who was not a Jew. The unconverted have no personal understanding of the significance of the broken body and shed blood of Christ. There has never been a time when they have been united with Him through faith. They have not become a part of His body. They have not been washed in His blood. For them, the celebration of the Lord's Supper is meaningless ritual.

The Word of God warns against unworthy participation in the Lord's Supper. Paul wrote: "For he that eateth and drinketh unworthily, eateth and drinketh damnation to himself, not discerning the Lord's body. For this cause many are weak and sickly among you, and many sleep" (1 Cor. 11:29,30). The teaching is clear, and very strong. There are those who have become sick, even died, as a result of unworthy participation in Holy Communion. They have eaten and drunk damnation to themselves because they were not able to comprehend the significance of the ordinance. Of course, we cannot expect them to. The

Lord's Supper is a spiritual feast. The unconverted are spiritually dead. They cannot comprehend spiritual matters. It is important for us to share with them the message of the gospel, but it is equally important that they not participate in the Lord's Supper until they have personally accepted the Christ who instituted that Supper. The ordinance of Holy Communion is a serious thing.

These warnings are directed to the man on the street who does not know Christ, the man who walks into a public service and receives Holy Communion because he happens to be seated in one of the pews when the Lord's Supper is served. Before he can receive that ordinance worthily he must be saved, he must be born again. Then, and only then, is he eligible to receive the feast that is served at the Lord's table. No strangers were permitted to receive the Passover feast. No strangers to the household of grace should be allowed to participate in the Lord's Supper.

The third restriction of the Passover involved leaven. At the time of Passover, Jews were not allowed to have leaven in their houses. This restriction did not refer to strangers and outsiders. Rather the participants were to light candles and thoroughly search their homes for any trace of leaven, or yeast. If any was found, it was to be taken out of the house and destroyed. The people were instructed to search their cupboards, their ovens, and places where the children might have laid a piece of bread. No leaven could remain in the house at the time of Passover.

In Scripture, leaven represents sin. Before we receive

the Lord's Supper we should repeat the diligent search the Jews carried out before Passover. Before participating in the memorial feast we should use the lighted candle of the Word of God and the searching flame of the Holy Spirit to uncover old leaven that may have cluttered our lives. We should dispose of the old leaven of unclean living, of worldliness, of hatred, lies, adulteries, and all other such personal sins. Remember, this purging of leaven was not for the strangers. It was the Jews who lived within the house who were to search out and remove the leaven. Those who would live under the covenant and blessing of God were required to purify their homes before God. Those of us who would enjoy the fellowship with Christ that is ours through Holy Communion must clean out of our lives those things that might separate us from God.

The period before the Passover was a time of preparation and self-examination. Such should be the case with the Lord's Supper. Everyone who would sit at the Lord's table should first examine his own life to be certain that he has fulfilled the Lord's requirements, that he has been born again, that he has been cut off from the old way of life, and that he has thoroughly purged himself of the leaven of sin that might hinder his fellowship with Christ and with the others who share the Lord's Supper.

4
The Two Cups of Communion

The cup is central to the Lord's Supper. An understanding of the cup is central to an understanding of the ordinance. Yet when we view the Lord's Supper, and the events it represents, we are drawn to the fact that in those final hours before Calvary there is not one cup, but two. There is the cup of the Lord, and there is the Lord's cup. There is the cup that Christ received from His Father, and there is the cup that we receive from Christ. There is the cup that He drank on our behalf, and there is the cup that we drink at His invitation. They are two, and yet the message of each is wondrously woven into the message of the other.

We read about the first of these cups in John 18:11. "Then said Jesus unto Peter, Put up thy sword into the sheath: the cup which my Father hath given me, shall I not drink it?" Here He was speaking of His own cup, the cup from which He would drink, the cup of the Lord. The second cup, the cup which He gives to us, is described in 1 Corinthians 11:25,26. "After the same manner he took the cup, when he had supped, saying, This cup is the new testament in my blood: this do ye, as oft as ye drink it, in remembrance of me.

For as often as ye eat this bread and drink this cup, ye do show the Lord's death till he come." Studying the two cups can help us understand the relationship we enjoy with Christ. In an earlier chapter we spoke a great deal of the union with Christ we enjoy through Holy Communion. When we understand the relationship of the two cups, we will better understand that union.

OUR CHRISTIAN INHERITANCE

There can be no better place to begin a study of our union with Christ than with the question "What is union?" *Union* is the condition that exists when one or more things are united. Being united is being bound together. When things are united they become less identifiable as individual things and more recognizable as one unit. When things come into union with each other they are no longer thought of principally as several small things, but as one larger thing.

Often, when a person accepts Christ as Savior and is born again he is elated at the knowledge that he will escape eternal judgment and be allowed everlasting sanctuary in heaven. But many times the new Christian does not realize all that has become his when he accepted Jesus. Sadly, that Christian may go through much, or all, of his life on earth without ever enjoying his salvation to its fullest, because he does not realize what became his at his new birth.

One of the purposes of the Lord's Supper is to remind us of these benefits. Without detracting from the beauty and splendor of heaven, we need to understand that escaping hell and gaining heaven is not all there is to salvation. Receiving a place in heaven is the result of the transaction that took place on our behalf at the moment we accepted Christ. Central to that transaction is our union with Him. When we accepted Christ, we were united with Him, bound to Him, literally placed in Him. All that we were was placed upon Him, and all that He is was made available to us. When a person is saved, he does not merely receive a ticket to heaven. Instead, he becomes the beneficiary of a divine plan that makes a life of victory on earth and an eternity of blessing in heaven the normal and expected things.

The whole process begins with a principle called imputation. Imputing is similar to an accounting transaction in which credit is applied to one's account, or expenses are charged to that account. If you were to go to a department store and buy an item with a credit card, the price of that item would be charged to your account. When payment came due, you would be required to either make payment or forfeit the item. Imagine, however, someone who knew and loved you entered the store and, from his own pocket, paid in full for the item which you had charged. Your account would be reduced to a zero balance, and no more would be required of you. The payment of another would have been credited, or imputed, to your account. It would be a senseless waste of time to suggest that since you had not personally made the payment some further payment was due from you. You would need only to display the

43

receipt, marked "PAID IN FULL," to silence any critic. This is the principle of imputation. Let us, then, examine how that principle applies to salvation.

All of us are descendants of Adam. When Adam rebelled against God, he died spiritually. That part of him which was able to enjoy the most intimate fellowship with God was rendered ineffective. All of us have inherited that defect. The question at hand is not whether we are good or bad, but whether we are descended from Adam. Even though evolutionary teaching has tried for generations to persuade us otherwise, we cannot escape the scriptural teaching that all of us are physically and spiritually tied to that first created man. We are, by nature, defective. We are sinners, because we were born that way. We cannot, by reformation or dedication, change that fact any more than a dog, by chirping, could become a bird, or a bird, by barking become a dog. We have inherited our nature from our father, Adam.

But we have inherited other things from Adam as well. Adam lived in a perfect environment. It was free from conflict, heartache, disease, pain, sorrow, and imperfection. When Adam sinned, not only did he die spiritually, but he also brought down God's wrath on all of creation. God cursed the earth because of Adam's sin. Beauty was replaced with barrenness. Harmony gave way to discord. Ease was pushed aside by labor. Perfection was marred by imperfection. Life withered into death. All the pain, all the sorrow, all the unpleasantness, all the death in our world can be traced either directly, or indirectly, to Adam's choice of sin and God's resulting curse.

44

Adam's sin effectively alienated him, and all his descendants, from God.

But God is a God of love. God judged Adam for his sin, but He did not cease to love the man He created. He thrust Adam out of the Garden, but He made him a coat of animal skin to cover his nakedness. God still loved Adam. Likewise, God loves the descendants of Adam. We do not deserve that love. We cannot earn it. Still, God offers it. Because He loves us, God has provided a means for restoring to us that which was lost in Adam. That process, that transaction, is very similar to the imaginary case of the department store charge account.

The simplest explanation is this: God "charged" all of our sin to Christ's account and all of Christ's righteousness to our account. All the penalty and judgment that our sin deserved was charged to Christ's account. He, then, paid that account in full with His broken body and shed blood. On the other side of the ledger, all that Christ accomplished through that sacrifice was credited to our account. There are many passages of Scripture that touch upon this marvelous transaction. Consider these few:

For the love of Christ constraineth us; because we thus judge, that if one died for all, then were all dead: And that he died for all, that they which live should not henceforth live unto themselves, but unto him which died for them, and rose again. . . . Therefore if any man be in Christ, he is a new creature: old things are passed away; behold, all things are become new. . . .

For he hath made him to be sin for us, who knew no sin; that we might be made the righteousness of God in him (2 Cor. 5:14,15,17,21).

Who his own self bare our sins in his own body on the tree, that we, being dead to sins, should live unto righteousness: by those stripes ye were healed (1 Pet. 2:24).

Surely he hath borne our griefs, and carried our sorrows: yet we did esteem him stricken, smitten of God, and afflicted. But he was wounded for our transgressions, he was bruised for our iniquities: the chastisement of our peace was upon him; and with his stripes we are healed. All we like sheep have gone astray; we have turned every one to his own way; and the LORD hath laid on him the iniquity of us all (Isa. 53:4-6).

What is it that these verses teach us? They tell us that everything we inherited from Adam went to the cross with Christ. All the tragic fruit of Adam's sin went up the road to Calvary with Jesus. He bore them in His own body. He bore all our sins. He bore our inherited position in Adam. He bore our curse, our griefs, our sorrows, our chastisement, our wounds, our bruises, and our iniquity. All that has come to us as the result of Adam's sin was borne by Jesus for us. It was all imputed to Him. It was all charged to His account. When the charges had been made, Christ paid them in full.

What are the benefits to us from this transaction? Imputation is a two-way transaction. What was charged against our account was imputed to Christ's. What was credited to Christ's account was imputed to ours. Every benefit obtained by Christ through His sacrifice on Calvary has already been written down on our side of the ledger. First, we understand that Christ accomplished death for us. The wages, or payment due us for our sin, is death. But Jesus has already satisfied that required payment.

Death is no longer a threat to us. It is as senseless for us to fear death as it would be for us to fear the collection agent in our department store illustration. All that was necessary to silence that agent was to display the paid receipt. In the case of death, the same is true. Christ's shed blood, represented to us by the cup of the Lord's Supper, is the receipt, the irrefutable evidence that death has been accomplished on our behalf. When Christ died, we died with Him. The demand for payment was satisfied. But Christ's death accomplished more for us than the mere satisfaction of the wages of sin. When Christ died, everything that He had borne up that gruesome hill died with Him. Our sins died with Him. Our curse died with Him. Our griefs died with Him. Our sorrows, chastisement, wounds, bruises, and iniquity all died with Him. These things should have no more power over us. They are dead. The Bible says they are dead. God considers them dead. All that remains is for us to, by faith, accept the fact that they are dead.

Death, however, is only half the picture. Christ died, then later rose from the dead. It only follows that if we were crucified with Christ, we were also made alive with Him. The old life, which was Adam's life, is dead. New life, which is God's, has been given to us. We are not changed; we are born all over again. We are new creatures. The old is gone, the new has come. All this is possible because of our union with Christ. When we accepted Christ as Savior, God placed us in Him. We are not beside Christ, or behind Him. We are *in* Him. We are united with Him. Because we are in Him, His death has become our death, and His resurrection has become our resurrection. All the things that were destroyed by His death were destroyed for us and in us. All the benefits of life that sprung forth from that borrowed tomb have become ours to claim.

THE CUP OF DEATH, THE CUP OF LIFE

All this, of course, brings us back to the matter of the two cups. Jesus drank of one. We drink of the other. One is horrible. One is marvelous. We deserve the horrid one, but Christ has already drunk of it for us, so we are now able to enjoy the marvelous cup. Each time we do, we are reminded of all that Christ accomplished for us. We are reminded that we are in Him and He in us.

The first cup, Christ's cup, pictures His sacrificial death. After celebrating the final Passover feast with His disciples, Christ entered the Garden of Gethsemane on the western slope of the Mount of Olives, a brief walk from the upper room. Kneeling under an olive tree, our Lord began to drink from His cup. What was the nature of that cup? His cup was a cup of bitter solitude, a cup of loneliness. His nearest disciples slept while He was in agony. Under that great rugged tree, He was alone. Shortly, even His heavenly Father would turn away. Jesus drank of the cup for you and me. When He had drunk all, He offered us a cup of friendship and fellowship. When we come to the Lord we receive the fellowship of the saints and the friendship of many wonderful brothers and sisters.

What a difference there is between His cup and ours! The cup He drank of was bitter, accompanied by loneliness and solitude. The cup we drink of is sweet with fellowship and friendship. I have heard thousands of people say that since they have come to the Lord they have enjoyed the sweetest moments of their lives. This is the cup of sweetness. We enter into fellowship and gladness with one another through Christ. Through Him we have become one with all others who believe in Him. There is no more need for loneliness or bitterness. He drank of that cup for us, so that we might enjoy a better one.

In drinking of His cup He has given us a different cup, a cup of fellowship with other believers and with the Lord.

The cup Jesus drank of was also a cup of betrayal. One with whom Jesus walked, with whom He had talked, with whom He had eaten, with whom He had climbed the rugged Judean hills was the one who turned on Him. One who had been present when Jesus healed the sick and raised the dead became the Lord's betrayer. It was a tragic and painful episode for Christ, yet it is so typical of life. Betrayal is often the rule, not the exception. The one whom we believe to be our nearest companion may turn farthest from us. We may be saddened, yet it should not be a time for despair. For at that exact moment God's Spirit may remind us that there is a Friend who sticks closer than a brother. That Friend is Jesus. He drank of a cup filled with betrayal so that He might offer us a cup of loyalty. During difficult times we may enter the very throne room of God, and come into the presence of the Most High, and He seems to say, "I have a cup for you, a cup of loyalty. I will not leave you. I will not forsake you. You will never be alone." We drink the cup of loyalty made available to us because Jesus endured one filled with betrayal.

Because of what Christ accomplished through His betrayal, death, and resurrection, we can enjoy a bond of loyalty foreign to nonbelievers. As a result of the new birth made possible by that betrayal, the Spirit of Christ is alive in us. That same Spirit is alive in our fellow believers. We are in Christ. They are in Christ. The result is a supernatural bond of fellowship stronger than anything else on earth. Sometimes our Christian friends become closer to us than our own families, and the friendship of those within the church stronger than the bond of blood relationship. This is the cup of loyalty. Christ is loyal to us. His servants are loyal to us. We are able to be loyal to Him and to all who are His.

As we look closer at the cup Jesus drank of, we see that it was a cup of anger, a cup of wrath. Many were angry with Him. Satan was angry with Him. Governmental officials were angry with Him. Religious people were angry with Him. This is sometimes a confusing situation. Jesus' greatest opposition came from those who should have recognized and supported Him. Often, those we would expect to be tender and kind are not so. Jesus had to suffer this. But Jesus faced more than mere human anger and betrayal. He faced the wrath of God. When He became sin for you and me, He was saying, "I accept Lester Sumrall's sins, and the sins of all mankind, and carry them with me to the cross." The Father's reply was clear: "I cannot look upon sin." The Bible tells us that the Father turned His back on Jesus, His only begotten Son. Jesus cried out, "My God, my God, why hast thou forsaken me?" (Matt. 27:46). In that moment Jesus was enduring the wrath of God against sin. In so doing, He was providing for us a cup of peace. He took to Himself the cup of wrath and anger so that He might present to us the cup of peace.

Peace is a gift from God. It is a fruit of the Holy Spirit's presence in our lives. We, as believers in Christ, do not seek peace. We *have* peace. It has been given to us. It flows outward from our innermost beings. We do not need to seek it, as the unbeliever does. Man may spend his fortunes, may run to the seashores or climb to the mountains seeking an elusive thing called peace. Christians do not need to launch such an ambitious and futile search. They need only to look to Jesus and accept the accomplished fact. As they receive the bread and the cup, they are reminded that Jesus suffered anger so that His people might know peace.

The cup Jesus drank of was a cup of bruisings. The Romans beat Him savagely with whips and with their hands. Scarlet furrows were cut into His flesh

51

by their cruel scourge. They forced a jagged crown of thorns down upon His brow. He drank long and deep from the cup of bruisings, that we might have a cup of healing. Isaiah wrote that by His stripes we are healed. Peter wrote that by His stripes we *were* healed. The use of the past tense there is not accidental. The healing has already been consummated. All that remains is for the believer to accept that accomplishment. The receiving of the Lord's Supper should be a time of healing. As believers receive the broken bread, they should be reminded that Christ's body was broken for their healing. That realization should quicken in them the faith necessary to step out and claim the healing that God has already accomplished on their behalf. It belongs to us. He has purchased it for us.

Christ's cup was also a cup of sorrows. Scripture calls Him a Man of sorrows. Yet most of those sorrows were ours, sorrows that He carried up Golgotha's hill for us. He bore them there so that we might have a cup of joy. Our sorrows became His sorrows so that His joy might become ours.

Finally, the cup which Jesus received from His Father was a cup of death. One of the most astounding facts of history is that God would be willing to die so that man might live. Jesus, who was in every way equal to God the Father, humbled Himself to the position of death. Jesus had no sin of His own but took on Himself our sins.

The Jews did not kill Jesus. Had He wished to escape them, He could have turned them away with one sweep of His hand. The Romans did not kill

Jesus. One word from His mouth could have called for such awesome legions of heavenly warriors that even the mighty armies of Rome would have cowered in retreat. Flesh and blood did not kill Jesus; sin killed Jesus. It was not His sin; it was *our* sin, yours and mine. Jesus, according to His own loving choice, voluntarily bore our sins, even though bearing them meant His own death. Jesus chose to drink of the cup of death so that we could drink from the cup of life. There is no more death for us. Christ has pressed that cup against His lips and drained it to the dregs. He bore death for us, so that we might never have to face it ourselves. The believer may have to face the shadow, or appearance, of death; but it is only a shadow, not death.

The earthly body, the flesh and blood that descended from Adam, may wither and fade, but the spirit, which is born again from God, cannot die. It will be united with a new and glorified body and will live forever in the presence of God Himself. When Jesus drank of the cup of death and then rose victoriously from the grave, He forever abolished death's reign of terror over the believer. He emptied the cup of death and replaced it with a cup of eternal life.

There are two cups involved in Holy Communion. Only one is visible to our physical eyes. It is the cup Christ gives us. It is a cup of fellowship and friendship, a cup of loyalty, of peace, healing, joy, and life. Yet it was only made possible because Jesus was willing to drink of a cup of bitterness and loneliness, solitude, betrayal, wrath, bruisings, sorrows, and death.

The Stigma of Calvary

The Lord's Supper, Holy Communion, is so much more than many believe. It is not a Sunday celebration. It is more; it is life. It is a reminder that Christ has made us one with Himself. It witnesses to us that we are in Christ and that He is in us. It brings to our minds all the things Jesus bore on our behalf and all the things He has made available to us.

5
Three Crosses

The Lord's Supper is necessarily linked to the death of Christ. The bread represents His broken body; the cup represents His shed blood. Any consideration of the Lord's Supper must focus to some degree on Calvary and the crucifixion of Christ.

Let us, then, study the Crucifixion by discussing three crosses. These are not the crosses that stood on the hill outside of Jerusalem. These are the crosses mentioned in Galatians 6:14. "But God forbid that I should glory, save in the cross of our Lord Jesus Christ, by whom the world is crucified unto me, and I unto the world."

The three crosses of which Paul spoke are, in fact, only one cross. Yet there are three distinct aspects of the work of that cross. In a sense, we do no injustice to Paul's writing to speak of three crosses.

CRUCIFYING SELF-GLORIFICATION

Paul desired that he should never glory, or boast, or find reason for pride, in anything but the cross of Jesus Christ. Paul's desire was to glorify Christ, not Paul. He meant that there should never be any self-glorification. How easy it is to place ourselves upon a pinnacle and feel that we are better than others, cleaner than others, or more holy than others! How easily we forget that any value we have, any cleanness, any holiness we have comes to us through Jesus Christ. Self-glorification is a terrible thing. It is a nonspiritual attitude. It says that what I am is of my own making. Such an attitude ignores the fact that we are descendants of Adam, men and women who are sinful and unrighteous by our very nature.

Paul chose to glory in nothing but the cross of Christ. Why the cross? Why not some other aspect of Christ's work? Paul chose the cross because it was at the cross that Paul, in Christ, was crucified. Remember, when we accept Christ we accept His death as our own death. When He died, all that we were in Adam died with Him. Our "old man," our old way of life, was crucified with Christ. Therefore, all the things in which we might find reason to glory have already been nailed to the cross of Christ.

If we quit looking at the cross, if we take our attention off of that cruel scene, we may not remember that we are crucified with Christ there. As long as we keep the cross before us, we are reminded that any reason for personal boasting was nailed to that Roman cross with Jesus. Again we see the value of the Lord's Supper. How can we possibly eat the bread and drink of the cup without being reminded that our old man is dead? There is no reason to glory in ourselves.

Still, self-glorification is common. It takes many forms. One form is race glorification. We frequently see people boasting of their particular race, implying that others are inferior in some way. One says, "I am black." Another boasts that he is not black. One boasts of his Asian heritage, while another is proud not to be of Asian descent. This is foolish. It is carnal. Race-glorification will never bring anyone to heaven. It is all for no reason. No race is superior or inferior to any other.

The blood that flows through our veins is the same, regardless of the pigment of our skin. The blood of an Asian can be used in a life-saving transfusion for a South American. The blood of a South American can save a European. The blood of a European can save an American Indian. The blood of an American Indian can save an African. From a purely natural sense, race-glorification is without basis. From a spiritual standpoint, it is even more unfounded. When Jesus went to the cross, all that we are died with Him, including our racial distinctions. The sins of men and women from all races sent Jesus to the cross, and the sins of men and women from all races died with Him there. He did not die for certain racial groupings. He died for everyone.

The important question is not whether we belong to a certain racial group, but whether we are in Christ.

When we come into union with Him, our individual racial heritage loses significance. This does not mean we should be ashamed of our racial heritage. We should not be ashamed to be black or white or yellow. This simply means racial heritage is irrelevant. In Christ we have a new racial heritage. We are the offspring of God, born into His family. There, the color of our skin is meaningless. The cross of Christ should be a constant reminder of that fact.

Another form of self-glorification is the glorification of nations. Often various nations will rise and boast that theirs is the greatest country. Whether they are French, German, Japanese, or American, this attitude is not pleasing to God. Paul said, "I will not glory in this." Understand that Paul had apparent reason for boasting. He was Roman, and being a Roman in those days was much like being an American today. Still, Paul chose not to boast of his national heritage. I am not suggesting that Christians be ashamed of their national heritage, that they refuse to salute their flag, or that they be disrespectful to their national leaders. I only wish to emphasize that there will be no ethnic neighborhoods in heaven. In Christ there are no national distinctions. We may thank God that we live in a country that, by His grace, allows greater liberty and more opportunity than another, but we must never lose sight of the truth that we have that liberty and opportunity only through God's grace.

We cannot glory in something that God has given us which we in no way earned. We may be grateful for our national heritage, but we should only glory in the cross of Christ.

There are many areas in which Christians continually glory and boast, when in fact there should be but one, the cross of Christ. There are those who boast and glory in their church. The local church is important;

we should support our church, love it, and be grateful for it. But our glorying should be in the cross of Christ.

Others boast of their education. Paul was an educated man. In fact, he was so well educated that one governor said that he had gone crazy because of too much learning. Still, Paul chose not to glory in his education, but only in the cross.

Others boast of their philosophy, traditions, rituals, or material possessions, but Paul decided to glory only in the cross of Christ. It was the cross that reminded Paul of the grace of God. It was the cross that reminded Paul that all his national heritage, racial heritage, education, philosophy, traditions, and all the advantages of this world had to offer could not bring him one step closer to God, or one foot nearer the gates of heaven.

Paul knew that long after race had been forgotten, nations had faded, education had ceased, traditions had vanished, and material wealth had decayed, the cross and the work that Jesus did there would remain. Paul had his emphasis in the proper place. He chose not to glory in those things that are temporary. He chose to glory in that which is eternal, the cross of Christ.

CRUCIFYING WORLDLINESS

Paul also said the world was crucified to him. This is another aspect of the cross. Paul developed a new viewpoint of this world. One of the major difficulties for many Christians was no problem for him. Many believers have no trouble loving Jesus. After all, He loved us and gave up all the wealth of heaven to bring us forgiveness and eternal life. But ceasing to love the world *is* a problem. We, as descendants of Adam, were born into this world. We grew up here and live here every day. The things we enjoy doing are found here. The people we love live here. We have no trouble loving God, but we just can't seem to let go of the *world*.

The real problem is that we cannot, or will not, distinguish between the temporal and eternal. We confuse temporary pleasures and values with eternal ones. We become spiritually cross-eyed, and our only cure is the cross. Paul identified those things that were temporary and nailed them to the tree. His attitude was, "The world is nailed to the tree like a criminal. The world is doomed. I will take the world, with all its rottenness, and nail it to the cross. It is crucified to me."

That was Paul's solution. It should be ours, too. Identify those things that are of this world and execute them on the cross.

Identifying the things that are of the world is a continuing process. On one day, the Holy Spirit may convict us that something is of the world. So we quickly take that thing and nail it to the cross. The next day, He may show us something entirely different that must go to that same cross. We shouldn't expect to put everything on that cross in one trip. Nor should we be discouraged if, just when we think the world's hold on us is dead, the Spirit shows us a new area that needs to be crucified. This is normal. It is part of spiritual growth.

We should not be discouraged if we cannot clearly identify all that needs crucifixion at any one moment, as long as we are always ready to crucify any form of worldliness that the Holy Spirit reveals to us. Identifying worldliness is really a matter of developing heavenly vision. We need to see things as God sees them. We need to look at things the way God does. Then the things of the world will become easily visible to us.

As descendants of Adam we were born into this world. However, we dare not forget that the cross of Christ has cancelled our inheritance from Adam, and the resurrection of Christ has given us a new birth. In a very real sense, we are no longer connected to this world. Our birth through Adam is done away with. Now we are born of God. All that we have as a result of our Adamic birth is only temporary. It can go to the cross.

We have said that we grew up here; that is partially true. Our physical bodies have experienced growth on this planet. Yet our physical body is part of the old birth. As newly born Christians, we began to experience spiritual growth. We are even now growing in the Lord. Our physical growth, our physical bodies, are temporary. They, and all their sickness and pain and imperfections, are not a part of God's new creation for us. They can go to the cross. We have said that we live here every day. That is true, as well, and the truth of it is a large part of our problem. In

Ephesians 2:6 Paul tells us that God has raised us up from spiritual death through Christ Jesus, and has elevated us to sit with Christ in heavenly places. In other words, our true position is in heaven. Our life is there. Our position here is only temporary.

For the next few years, and none of us can be certain how many, our day-to-day activity will be limited to this world. But our life is not of this world; our life is heavenly. In a short time, whether through physical death or at the return of Christ, our temporary existence here will give place to our permanent existence with Christ in heavenly places. We have also said that the things we enjoyed doing are here. Can you imagine Paul at the Roman Colosseum watching a gladiator contest? What Rome considered the choicest pleasure, Paul considered vile and depraved. He nailed it to the cross. The popular pleasures of this day would sicken Paul. Ours is a world eaten up by pleasure. Like the Romans of two thousand years ago, we live for enjoyment. Yet these senseless frivolities last only a few moments. They bring us temporary pleasure, and whet our sensual appetites for even more. These temporary pleasures must go to the cross.

I am not suggesting that all enjoyment is wrong, though some forms of enjoyment most definitely are. I believe that Paul enjoyed frequent moments of clean and wholesome pleasure. But even these wholesome things were temporary. They did not control Paul, nor did he live for them. He was willing to lay even the harmless pleasures aside if God required it. All of this world was crucified to him.

Finally, we have said that the people we love live in this world. One of the things that makes heaven near and dear to us is the knowledge that many of our friends and loved ones are already there. We are drawn to that place because it is where people we love are living. We have already seen that those of us who are in Christ are not of this world. Our physical being exists here temporarily, but our life is in heaven. The same is true of our friends and neighbors who have accepted Christ but have not yet gone on to meet Him. In that sense, the people we love do not live here. Some of them have already transferred their resident status to heaven. Others, though waiting to make that transfer, have not yet departed. It is of little consequence whether we go before them or they before us. Eventually we will all be united in that glorious place.

The element of sadness enters in the fact that many whom we love are neither living in heaven nor waiting to move there. They are lost and without hope. They, too, just like every other thing that is of this earth, must be taken to the cross. There are two dimensions, two ways, in which we must place them there.

First, we must realize that only God can save them. Our righteousness cannot save them, and theirs certainly cannot. So in prayer we must take them to the cross. We must say, "I love these people, and I know that You do also. I cannot save them. You can. Please, by Your Holy Spirit, show them they need salvation and bring them to a place of accepting Christ." We cannot die for them; Christ already has. Therefore, we must take them to His cross in prayer.

Still, there is a second way in which we can take them to the cross. That way is the gospel. We may speak to them personally about Christ; we may invite them to attend a gospel service; we may give them good books or gospel tracts; we may direct their attention to Christian radio or television broadcasts. There are many paths down which we may lead them, so long as those paths end at the cross.

CRUCIFYING SELF

Not only did Paul regard the world as dead and gone, he also considered himself as dead to the world. Paul, as a believer, was crucified with Christ. When Christ went to the cross, Paul went too. When Christ died, Paul died. What good are the things of this world to a dead man? They are of absolutely no value. Before his conversion, Paul was rapidly advancing in the religious system of his day. He was a Pharisee. He was zealous. He had studied under the greatest teachers of the time. His future was bright. He had ambition and potential. But Paul never fulfilled that ambition or realized that potential. Just when he seemed near to reaching the height of success within the Jewish religion, Paul "died." How many times have we heard of or read about a promising young man or woman who has been cut down in their prime by death? It seems such a tragedy. In Paul's case, however, it was not. Paul was filled with promise and was at his prime. But his death was no tragedy; it was a victory.

Saul of Tarsus left Jerusalem enroute to Damascus. He had official papers from the high priest. He was going to take some Christians into custody. At some point along that road, Saul of Tarsus came face to face with Jesus of Nazareth. And Saul of Tarsus died. His body did not cease to function, and his heart did not stop. He did not quit breathing. But he died, nonetheless. He was no longer advancing in the religious system of his day. He was no longer a Pharisee. He was no longer ambitious or zealous. His future no longer held the promise of popularity among his fellows. In fact, he was no longer even Saul of Tarsus. He was crucified with Christ, and the old way of life was gone.

How beautiful this is, how lovely! Here is a man who chose to identify himself with all the suffering and giving of Christ, even though it meant the end of all that had once seemed important. Those of you who have lived enough years have watched bright young stars appear in the entertainment industry, sparkle for a brief time, then vanish. You have beheld the fallen stars of the financial world. But Paul shows us a better way. It is better for you and me to be crucified with Christ than for us to live a flagrant life of sin and pleasure, only to die and be eternally lost.

Paul could have been someone important in the eyes of the world, yet he chose to die. He chose to allow his plans and dreams to be crucified with Christ. He chose to become a nobody. To those of his time, he wasted his life on a poor cause. He went from potential to oblivion. Yet in a way that few could have foreseen, God elevated Paul to a position of spiritual prominence that no one outside of Christ Himself has ever enjoyed. Paul gave up everything. He willingly became a nobody. Because of that attitude God made him somebody very special.

This world had no place for Paul. Though he had once been important in it, he said, "I want no place in this world." To many, that seems like an old-fashioned idea, a dead puritanism. But it is not. There are young men and women rising up today with a greater desire and willingness to abandon all and go to the cross with Jesus than this world has ever known. There are young people within the church who have more desire to sacrifice themselves in order to save the world than we have had in many generations. This is thrilling. Yet there are still so many to whom religion is comfortable and cozy. They know of no death to the old way, no sacrifice, no crucifixion. The church, especially in America, has become luxurious and lazy. We have many million-dollar, and even multimillion-dollar, churches. Yet half the people living on earth have never ever heard the name Jesus, much less the wonderful truth that He will forgive their sins and give them eternal life.

We have not carried out the Great Commission. We have not given the gospel to our generation. We sit in our expensive buildings, our gorgeous carpets beneath our feet, our magnificent stained-glass windows filtering the rays of light, our glorious pulpits before us, our inspiring choirs entertaining us. We glitter with our own glamor, but our spirits are not at the cross where Jesus died.

Jesus had to die, or we could not be saved. There is no salvation apart from the cross of Christ. Christ, the Son of God, came from a resplendent throne in heaven, surrounded by tens of thousands of angels who constantly sang His praises, in order to face the cross for you and me. He accomplished on our behalf all that God requires in order for us to enter into His presence. His cross, His work was sufficient to do that which nothing else could do. For that reason Paul chose to glory in nothing but Christ's cross. He said, "I will nail the world to the cross. It is dead to me." Further, he said, "I will go to that cross, as well." I do not know many people who are, at this moment, crucified to this world. They glory in their big cars, beautiful homes, and prestigious careers. They cannot say with Paul, "The world is crucified to me, and I unto the world."

As we take Communion we should be impressed with the need of adopting Paul's attitude. The bread is broken. So should our lives be broken, not torn to pieces by sin, but humbled by the grace of God. We should allow our hearts to be broken with the burden that Paul carried for the salvation of the world. Our hearts should be broken for the thousands who die each day, for the millions who are hungry, for the multitudes who suffer from disease or distress.

As we take that broken bread we should ask God to break our will, our pride, our self-righteous attitudes, even as the body of His only begotten Son was broken for us. That bread should forever remind us of the attitude we, as believers, should always display toward those around us. As that bread is broken, as Christ was broken, so should we be broken also.

When we drink of the cup, we should recall the blood that Jesus gave for us. Three thousand years before science had unlocked the mysterious functions of the bloodstream, Scripture told us blood is the source of life. Since the day of Adam, blood has been the price paid for sin. Blood speaks of atonement for sins. Blood should be our reminder of the means whereby we have a hope of heaven, and the responsibility that we have to share that hope with the world.

Three crosses were erected outside Jerusalem on the day Christ was crucified. On one cross a man died in sin, the thief who would not believe. On the middle cross a Man died for sin, paying the price required for the salvation of the world. On the third cross a man died to sin, gaining eternal life through faith in Christ. Those three crosses speak to us of rejection, redemption, and reception.

The first man rejected the message and was lost. The second Man *was* the message, giving Himself for the sins of others. The third man received the message and was saved. My first concern is that everyone who reads these pages be like that third man, who received Christ as Savior. I can only pray and hope that anyone reading these words who has not received Christ would do as that dying thief, and place all hope for eternity in Jesus Christ.

Many who read these pages have long ago placed their trust in Christ. Of them I would ask whether the three aspects of the cross that became so real to Paul have become real to them, too. How many of us can honestly say that we glory, or boast, in nothing but Christ's cross? How many of us can say that the world is dead, that it holds no pull or fascination for us? How many can say that they are dead to the world, that they have lain aside all their hopes, dreams, ambitions, family, material wealth, and job and life, itself, in order to serve Christ?

The next time we receive the Lord's Supper, the next time we partake of the broken bread and the cup, may we hear the words of Paul again: "But God forbid that I should glory, save in the cross of our Lord Jesus Christ, by whom the world is crucified unto me, and I unto the world."

6
The Sins That Killed Jesus

Receiving the Lord's Supper will to us always be a call to return to the scene of the Crucifixion. The bread and cup are memorials of that event. As we recall the cross, and the terrible picture it presents, we may experience anger, even rage, at the men who shed the blood of heaven's purest Gift to man. We may wonder what could bring people to commit such a heinous crime. But we need look no further than our own selves, no deeper than the contents of our own hearts; for there we find the same sinful motivations that drove the crowd of Jesus' day to crucify the very Lord of glory.

The writer of Hebrews notes, "For it is impossible . . . if they shall fall away, to renew them again unto repentance; seeing they crucify to themselves the Son of God afresh, and put him to an open shame" (Heb. 6:4,6). These verses have stirred a great deal of controversy through the years. It is not our purpose here to settle those controversies. We will deal instead with the concept that, being guilty of the sins that led to Christ's crucifixion, we are just as guilty as the crowd that nailed Him to the cross. In a real sense, our sins crucify Him afresh, for we renew in

71

Him the pain and broken heart that He suffered at Calvary. When we continually practice the sins that nailed Jesus to the cross, we are guilty of breaking that sinless body and shedding that innocent blood. What, you may wonder, are those sins? I believe them to be pride, greed, a vacillating mind, the fear of people, lustful desires, indifference to justice, and blind obedience to earthly authority.

It is true that the total sins of all of mankind, past, present, and future, killed Jesus; but it was these seven sins that seemed most obvious at His death.

PRIDE

Let us look at Caiaphas, the high priest. He was one of the men who accused Jesus and called for His crucifixion. We read of him, and his father-in-law Annas, in Luke 3:2, John 11:49, and Acts 4:6. These men were the chief religious leaders of the day. They were men of pride who allowed their position to cloud their judgment. They became so proud of themselves and the office they held that they were automatically opposed to anyone or anything that threatened their religious leadership. Jesus was such a threat.

They considered themselves great men and were quick to judge the unrighteousness of the common people. By contrast, Jesus was a humble man who called these religious leaders snakes and hypocrites. He told the people that their religion was worthless. In its place He offered them more than mere religion. He offered them life, and many people received it. The hearts of Caiaphas and Annas were filled with pride. Jesus had become too popular with the people for their liking. Deep within the hearts of these who claimed to be men of God, pride was stirring up a tempest of jealousy and an ocean of anger.

If we listen closely we can almost hear them speaking. "We cannot allow this upstart, this uneducated Galilean, this son of a carpenter to take our places. We are chief among the leaders of Israel. We know the law. No one else is better qualified to lead the people than we." Their pride killed Jesus. Their pride would not accept Him. Their pride would not acknowledge that His message was correct.

If we have pride, we are no better than they. Jesus says we are lost in sin and must be redeemed; having been redeemed, we must depend upon Him in everything. Our pride says that we are not quite so bad as all that, and that we are able to make it on our own in most cases. Our pride will not surrender completely to His leadership. Our pride will not admit that He is always right and we are in all ways wrong. Our pride has killed Him as surely as did the pride of Caiaphas and Annas. That same pride hurts Him every time it wells up in our hearts.

GREED

The second sin, greed, is pictured for us by Judas Iscariot. In Matthew 26:14-16 we read: "Then one of the twelve, called Judas Iscariot, went unto the chief priests, And said unto them, What will ye give me, and I will deliver him unto you? And they covenanted with him for thirty pieces of silver. And from that time he sought opportunity to betray him." I do not believe that Judas really hated Jesus. I think Judas loved Jesus in his own way. I am not trying to gloss over the terrible nature of Judas' sin, but only to emphasize that it was greed, rather than hatred, that led Judas to betray Christ.

I think that in his own mind Judas supposed Jesus would escape. He had seen Christ escape on other occasions; perhaps he thought Jesus would escape again. Or perhaps Judas was a little impatient for the kingdom Jesus had promised and thought that by bringing about His arrest he could force Jesus' hand, compelling Him to establish His earthly kingdom without delay. In any case, greed was the major motivator. As irrational and callous as such a scheme appears, it must have seemed to Judas an easy way to make a few dollars. Greed has that effect on people. It causes them to draw wrong conclusions and make false assumptions. When the opportunity for gain rears its head, reason, common sense, and integrity often flee. Greed is a powerful and driving force, so powerful it crucified Jesus Christ. If we are guilty of greed, we should come humbly to Christ, saying, "Take this greed away. I do not want to be one of those who would crucify You afresh and put You to open shame."

DOUBLEMINDEDNESS

The third sin that led to the death of Christ was vacillation, or doublemindedness. This sin is pictured for us in the life of Simon Peter. He said, "I will always be with You, Lord. When all others desert you, I will still be by your side." Sometimes boasting can be a terrible thing. We should always be careful not to boast of something we cannot perform. Peter talked a good religion, but when the trials came he was the first to run. When a young girl said to him, "I saw you with Jesus," Peter denied it. "No," he retorted, "that was not me. It was somebody else who must have looked like me." Another person spoke up. "But you are a Galilean. You do not belong here in Judea. Your speech tells us where you come from."

Faced with the prospect of being linked with the man whom the crowds sought to destroy, Peter began to vacillate. First, he was, then he was not. First he was Jesus' most loyal supporter, then he did not know Him at all. Peter cursed. He blasphemed God. His vacillating mind helped send Jesus to the cross. If we vacillate between serving and not serving God, we are as guilty as Peter. Vacillation is a terrible thing. Christians must not be this way one moment and that way the next. By God's grace and with His strength, we must learn to stand steadfastly on the side of the Lord Jesus Christ.

FEAR

Fear is the sin that Pontius Pilate adds to our roll. He feared the people who gathered in the streets. He feared the political power they represented. "You are not a friend of Caesar," they cried, "if you will not put to death this man who claims to be king." He looked at those people screaming and yelling and shaking their fists, and he who was supposed to be the judge began to tremble. He was not governed by reason or law. Pilate was governed by fear.

Fear, particularly fear of what others will say or think, is devastating. If you are governed by fear, you may do all sorts of insane things. Reason will flee, security will abandon you, and paranoia will become your constant companion. You will go through life always looking over your shoulder, weighing decisions not on the basis of right and wrong, but on the basis of possible harm to yourself. Fear will fill your life with wrong decisions, just as it drove Pilate to condemn Jesus to death.

Fear has no place in the heart of the Christian: ". . . perfect love casteth out fear" (1 John 4:18). We can know that perfect love in the Person of Jesus Christ. If you are ruled by fear, claim victory over it through Christ. Ask God's Holy Spirit to replace that fear with boldness. Do not allow yourself to be dominated by the sin that led Pilate to crucify Christ. Do not let fear cause you to crucify Him anew.

LUST

Lustful desire, adultery, was the fifth of the sins that nailed Jesus to the cross. It is presented to us in a curious fashion by Herod. Herod was an adulterer. He lusted for the wife of his brother, Philip, so he took her. When John the Baptist courageously denounced that sin, Herod had the preacher put to death. But the ruler's conscience never gave him ease. Matthew tells us that when Jesus launched His public ministry and began to become popular thoughout the country, Herod feared that John had in some way returned from the dead. Herod was in Jerusalem the night Jesus was brought before Pilate. Pilate, fearful and anxious to pass responsibility for Jesus to another, sent the Lord to be judged by Herod. In Luke 23:11,12 we read: "And Herod with his men of war set him at nought, and mocked him, and arrayed him in a gorgeous robe, and sent him again to Pilate. And the same day Pilate and Herod were made friends together: for before they were at enmity between themselves."

One preacher had condemned Herod's adultery and been executed. Now another preacher had arisen who was all too similar, in Herod's eyes, to the one who was dead. Herod wanted this one out of the way as well. Sometimes, in an effort to cover our own filthy sins, we destroy other people. That is what Herod did. His lustful adultery caused him to desire Jesus' death. This man's life had an awful ending. He was banished to Gaul, where he died alone. The woman whom he had taken unrighteously was not with him then. He made a mockery of Christ and took part in His death; but he, himself, met a lonely and fearful death.

Adultery and lust are awful things. Those who would participate in them virtually guarantee injury and heartache to themselves and to their friends and families. The sin of adultery helped drive Jesus to the cross, and that sin is still renewing the agony of Calvary in Him. When God's people fall into adultery, whether in the physical realm or in the secret brothels of the heart, they are guilty again of the blood of Christ.

INDIFFERENCE

There was a great crowd at the scene of Christ's death, and their sin and indifference also forced Jesus to the cross. They were a motley crowd, always present, never thinking. An individual may have definite opinions when he is alone, but when he is with ten people, his thinking may be swayed. He thinks still another way when drawn into a crowd of one hundred people. In a crowd of one thousand his thinking may change even more. His individuality grows less distinct. He begins to conform to the feelings and thoughts and words of the crowd. In such a crowd, no one person must bear the full weight of responsibility. No one person can be held responsible for the actions of the group. Normal restraint breaks down. Right and wrong are swallowed by a gray cloud of momentary expedience. No one can be held responsible, so no one cares.

This is indifference, mass indifference to justice and right. One voice cries out, "Crucify him!" Another echoes, "Crucify him!" A third picks up the call, and before long a mob of men and women, who under other circumstances might be calm and rational individuals, are chanting for the execution of an innocent man. They are totally indifferent to whether or not he is guilty. The crowd is calling for his death, so there must be a cause.

It is easy to be part of the crowd, to do what the

crowd does, to go where the crowd goes, to approve what the crowd approves. God, however, does not want us to be just another face in the crowd. He does not want us to stand by with an indifferent attitude toward the world around us. He does not want us to be swept along by the masses. God does not want us to crucify His Son afresh through our indifference to sin and to the needs of our fellow men. God wants us to stand firmly on the side of right, to care, to be grieved over wrong, even if it means turning our backs on the crowd and standing alone.

BLIND OBEDIENCE

The seventh sin that killed Jesus was blind obedience. This sin is represented for us by the Roman soldiers. They said, "If Rome says to do it, it will be done!" Right or wrong had nothing to do with their decision. They were not concerned with whether or not Jesus was a good man. Rome, through its representative Pilate, had said that Jesus should die. In blind obedience, those soldiers were willing to go to hell with Rome. It was not the first time blind obedience had destroyed men's moral integrity, nor will it be the last time.

It is often more convenient to be subservient to dictatorial rule. Blind obedience requires no courage. Many cowards, after slaughtering millions of Jews in Nazi Germany, said, "I did not kill without orders." Wrong is wrong, orders or no orders. Moral integrity would say, "Shoot me first. I will die, but I will not murder innocent people." When we stand before God

we will not be able to say, "I was with this government," or "I was with that government." We will not
be able to say, "I was only following orders." God will
respond, "I gave you a conscience. I gave you moral
teachers. I gave you a Bible filled with clear explana-
tions of right and wrong. I gave you a choice. You
should have made the right choice and been willing to
die by it."

God does not want anyone to walk in blind obedience. In many ways the men who killed Jesus were
not very different from men and women of our day.
In their blind obedience they were saying, "I am in
the great Roman army. We are the greatest army on
earth. When the emperor speaks, we obey. Governor
Pilate is the voice of the emperor. We will obey him.
Jesus, we do not know who You are. We have never
seen You before. But we know one thing, we are
going to nail You to a cross."

Many people, perhaps someone you know, perhaps
someone reading these pages, will go to hell in blind
obedience. If the boss says to tell a lie for the convenience of the company, they lie. If a strange woman
calls on them to commit adultery, they obey and
sacrifice their virtue. If friends or acquaintances
invite them to sin, they rush to it in blind obedience.
Wrong is wrong, and the orders of others are no
excuse. When we blindly obey those who would have
us do wrong, we are as guilty as the Roman soldiers
who nailed Jesus to the cross. It is wrong to obey
wrong orders. Believers should obey God. They should
obey the Bible, and turn their backs on orders that
would lead them into sin.

The Sins That Killed Jesus

What nailed Jesus to the cross? These seven things: pride, greed, a vacillating mind, fear of people, lustful desires, indifference to justice, and blind obedience. These same seven sins, when they are evident in the lives of believers, still contribute to the pain of Calvary. Believers who practice these sins are guilty of the blood of Christ. They are guilty of crucifying Him anew.

First there is *pride*, which says, "I am more important than anyone else. My needs are more important. My position is more important. I will not allow anyone to interfere with my comfort and convenience. If necessary, I will cut them down, cause them pain, embarrass them, or even kill them."

Second is *greed*, which says, "Give me more. Fill my bag. I cannot get enough. I cannot be satisfied." How many go to hell over greed! How many nail the Lord to the cross again through their desire to have more.

A *vacillating mind* is the third great killer. Its victim is faithful to Jesus on one day, and disobedient to Him the next. That sort of vacillation nails Him to the cross over and over again. Christians should place absolute trust in Christ and be steadfast. The Bible teaches us that an unstable person is like the sea, its waves swelling up and then falling away. Such an individual is unreliable and cannot be useful to God. He expects His people to be as strong as Gibraltar, as unmovable as a mountain. That kind of strength can only come through a consistent, nonvacillating trust in Jesus Christ.

Fear of people, the fourth sin, is the thief of opportunity. A world troubled on every side, trembling at the threat of nuclear war, buried under runaway inflation, and teeming with unloved souls, is crying out in hunger for purpose. Christians have that purpose. In Christ we have direction and life. We have the opportunity to steer many people to the feet of Jesus. But fear often robs us of that opportunity. Fear of people, fear of what they may think or say, keeps us from walking consistently in their sight. Fear keeps us from displaying a genuine testimony. Fear keeps us from leading them to Jesus. Fear of people crucified Christ; we dare not allow it to put Him to open shame again.

Lustful desires are the fifth sin that killed Jesus. Have you permitted your body and your desires to go wrong? Herod did, and the result was the crucifixion of Christ. Lust is like a cancer. It demands fulfillment, and is so strong that it will force aside anything that would postpone that fulfillment. Lust will cause an individual to mock righteousness, modesty, and morality. But like cancer, lust will bring destruction and death.

The sixth sin, *indifference*, affects the multitudes. The greatest number of people at the cross were the indifferent crowd. Indifference is being not overly concerned with the events surrounding us, as long as our own comfort and convenience are not disturbed. Indifference is the foundry where the chains of bondage are forged. Indifference is the key that opens the Pandora's box of bondage and slavery. Indifference is the iceberg that looms hidden beneath the waves until it can tear open the hold of the ship of state and sink forever liberty and freedom. Indifferent people are easy prey for slavery.

Christians should not be indifferent to the affairs of their church, to the needs of their pastor, or to the spiritual and moral fiber of their society. Do not think our world is improving. Do not think that the cesspool of Hollywood entertainment is becoming purer. Do not think that the problems of our educational system will go away by themselves. Do not assume that morality and integrity are automatically a part of the political system in a free country. Do not sit by in indifference, thinking that someone else will tend to the needs of the church, the pastor, the community, the schools, or the government. Do not assume that someone else will take a stand. Such indifference killed Jesus.

The final sin that crucified Jesus was *blind obedience* to the ungodly. God created men as individuals, and men will be judged as individuals. No one will be able to hide behind someone else's orders. It is better to face inconvenience, embarrassment, the loss of a job, even death, than to carry out wrong orders in the name of blind obedience.

These seven sins were apparent on the day of Christ's crucifixion. They are equally apparent today. When we are guilty of these sins, we crucify to ourselves the Son of God afresh and put Him to open shame. God has gone to great lengths to see that we do not forget the crucifixion of His Son. He has arranged a memorial supper for us, Holy Communion.

He has given us broken bread, which represents

the broken body of Jesus. He has given us a cup, which shows us His blood. He does not want us to forget. We cannot remember Calvary without remembering the pride of the high priest and of the Pharisees. We cannot remember Calvary without remembering the greed of Judas, the vacillating mind of Peter, the fear of Pilate, the lust of Herod, the indifference of the crowds, or the blind obedience of the Roman soldiers. We cannot remember Calvary without remembering the sins that drove Jesus there.

As we receive the bread and the cup, we should remember Calvary and the sins that made Calvary a necessity. Can we take that bread and that cup, can we recall the Crucifixion without examining our own lives to determine whether or not we are guilty of that broken body and that shed blood? As we partake of Holy Communion, may we always be reminded not only of the crucifixion of Christ, but also of the importance of living a righteous and holy life before God.

7

Seven Sayings, Seven Affirmations, Seven Words

Probably the most important six hours in the history of the world were the hours Christ spent upon the cross. Their significance touches three dimensions: heaven, earth, and hell. Deity, humanity, and the demonic forces of the underworld were locked in conflict. Into those few hours were packed the fulfillment of many Old Testament prophecies. In those brief hours God's centuries-old plan for the redemption of mankind was carried out. Everything about Christ's final day is significant. Every event that surrounded the crucifixion of Christ is significant for all eternity. All the words of Jesus are important, but the words He spoke on that day are given special meaning by the events of those hours.

SEVEN WORDS

Scripture records seven times when Jesus spoke from the cross. Each of these seven sayings gives us important insight into the work He performed for us there. The first of these sayings is found in Luke 23:34: "Then said Jesus, Father, forgive them; for they know not what they do."

His second statement is found in verse 43: ". . . Verily I say unto thee, To day shalt thou be with me in paradise."

His third statement from the cross is found in John 19:26: ". . . Woman, behold thy son!" Verse 27 continues the statement: ". . . Behold thy mother!"

The fourth saying of Jesus from the cross is found in Mark 15:34: ". . . My God, my God, why hast thou forsaken me?"

The fifth saying, found in John 19:28, is ". . . I thirst."

The sixth saying, found in verse 30, is ". . . It is finished . . ."

Christ's final words from the cross are found in Luke 23:46: ". . . Father, into thy hands I commend my spirit . . ."

We believe that the seven sayings from the cross represent seven ways in which Christ meets the needs of humanity. The first statement speaks of forgiveness. Jesus said, "Father, forgive them." Man needs that forgiveness. At the cross of Christ there was, and is, forgiveness, first and foremost.

The cross also shows us the authority of Christ to save. When the dying thief asked Jesus for salvation, Jesus gave it. There was no debate. There was no consideration. Jesus did not say, "Now, wait just a moment. Let Me ask My heavenly Father if there is any salvation for you. After all, you are almost in hell. I may not be able to save you now. You have been bad so long." No! The second statement of Jesus from the cross speaks to us of the authority of Christ to save. Jesus told the dying man that the two of them would be united in paradise that very day. The second statement from the cross is a positive and authoritative declaration of the power of Jesus Christ.

In the third statement from the cross we see compassion, responsibility, and remembrance. Jesus looked down from the cross at Mary. In the midst of all His pain and suffering, He had compassion for her. He realized His earthly responsibility to her. He remembered her and thought more of her than of Himself. Mary, apparently a widow by this time, faced double difficulties. Not only was she a widow in an age when women had a difficult time fending for themselves, she was also the mother of a Man who had been publicly executed as a criminal. She faced financial difficulty and public shame. Jesus, when He saw her, hurt for her. In ancient Jewish society the eldest son in the family became responsible for the well-being of his mother upon the death of his father. Joseph, Jesus' earthly father, was no longer in the picture. Jesus Himself would no longer be able to take care of His mother's earthly needs in the way He once had.

John, the disciple whom Jesus loved, His dear friend and comrade, was standing close by. Jesus looked to His mother and said, "Woman, behold thy son." In these words he was saying to his mother, "From now on, John will fulfill the needs that I once met for you. He will take care of you. He will see that you have the necessities of life."

Then He looked at John and spoke: "Behold thy mother." In those words He was saying, "John, if you are My friend, if you are My disciple, take care of this woman who brought Me into the world and reared Me in a godly home. Do not leave her without support."

Even at the cross Christ remembered the weak. He remembered His responsibility to others. He had compassion for those who needed His help. Many people in pain, waiting to die, are concerned only with their own well-being. Most would not devote their last ounce of energy to meet the needs of others. But Jesus did. Even in death, He could not forget the need He saw before Him.

The fourth statement of Christ from the cross was one of agony. He cried out, "My God, my God, why hast thou forsaken me?" Here is the ultimate in submission. Here is divine submission to death on the cross. Jesus was willing to do anything, everything that the Father wished Him to do. He was suffering agony, even separation from His heavenly Father, but was still submitting to His Father's divine authority. As God, Jesus died only because He allowed men to take His life. At any moment it was within His power to call upon the power of heaven for His rescue. He chose not to. Instead, He was submissive to the death of the cross.

He bore your sins and mine, and those sins separated Him from His heavenly Father. He had done nothing amiss. He had committed no crime. He was guilty of no sin. Still He faced separation from God for our sake. His conduct displays for us true submission. He could have escaped the cross but for our sakes chose not to. From darkened Calvary He cried out in agony but did nothing to relieve that agony. Escape was within His own power, but He submitted to the cross for you and me.

Christ's separation from His heavenly Father was a spiritual separation. When the sins of mankind were poured on Jesus, His soul and spirit were separated from God by those sins. God the Father could not, and would not look upon or tolerate sin. When the sins of the world were placed upon His Son, God turned His back upon Jesus. The result was great spiritual agony for Christ. His fourth statement reflects that.

His fifth saying from the cross reveals physical agony. He said, "I thirst." So many of us would like to sail through life on a flowery bed of ease, with no briars, no pain, no sorrow. Life is not that way. Even God's perfect Man suffered physical need. He experienced physical agony at Calvary. This fact should be an encouragement to us. In moments of despair and physical pain, we can seek comfort in the knowledge that our Lord Jesus experienced physical pain, too.

There were times when His body cried out for refreshment. There were times when His body longed for relief. There were times when His body ached. He understands our physical needs and is willing and able to help us with them. If we can learn anything from the fifth saying from the cross it is that God understands and is willing to help us, if we rely on Him. The fifth saying speaks not only of the momentary agony that Jesus experienced but also of His everlasting willingness to stand by us and help us in our own moments of agony.

In His sixth statement, Jesus was declaring the ultimate victory of the cross. When He proclaimed, "It is finished," He was not declaring that His death had come. Rather, He was saying that ultimate victory had been accomplished. He had brought salvation to the human race. He had paid the price for the sins of mankind. He had undone all that Adam had done four thousand years before. He had repaired the breach that Adam had made and had become the bridge from sinful human degradation to eternal life. Jesus knew His goal had been accomplished. The ultimate victory was His.

In His seventh statement Jesus said, with eternal confidence and trust, "Into thy hands I commend my spirit." He was to be united with His Father forever, never again to be separated. His final statement, and the attitude behind it, should picture for us the confident rest every believer can enjoy. We can know, because of the work Christ accomplished on the cross, that our spirit, our eternal welfare, is forever in the loving hands of our heavenly Father. Because of the work of Christ, there need never be a time when we are separated from God. There will never be a time when God will turn His back upon us. We are His forever.

SEVEN AFFIRMATIONS

In studying these seven statements, it may be useful to think of them as seven affirmations, seven times when Jesus affirmed very important truths for us. The first we shall call the *Affirmation of Propitiation.*

You recall from an earlier chapter that propitiation speaks of the satisfaction of a demand. The sin of mankind demanded payment. Jesus satisfied that demand, and knew that He had satisfied it. That is why, speaking from the cross, He asked His Father to forgive those who were crucifying Him. He was saying, for all time and eternity to hear, "I have satisfied the demand. Father, do not judge these people on the basis of what they are doing. Judge them on the basis of what I have done." God made a demand, and Jesus met it. Therefore, for all eternity, man can be judged on the basis of Christ's work, not man's own.

Of course, in order to take advantage of Christ's work for us, we must accept Him as Savior and Lord. When we do, we accept His payment as being sufficient for our sins. His statement from the cross affirmed for us and for His heavenly Father that He had satisfied, that He had become the propitiation for our sins.

The first statement was directed toward His Father. The second statement was directed toward a repentant sinner. Just as the first statement tells us that the demand for our sins has been satisfied, the second statement affirms to us that Jesus is willing to forgive. When Jesus told the dying criminal that he would be with Him in paradise that very day, He was affirming the reality of personal forgiveness and pardon.

In His dying hours Jesus provided for the needs of His mother. In so doing, He was affirming His intention to provide for our needs. From that day until the present Christ has been, and will continue to be, sufficient for our needs. His principal concern is for our spiritual well-being, but He is also concerned with our daily needs. He welcomes our requests. He who clothes the lilies of the field and cares for the fallen sparrows knows of our needs and is able to meet them. He welcomes us when we come before Him with our prayers and supplications. He has affirmed to us His desire to provide for those needs.

The fourth saying of Christ from the cross is the *Affirmation of Atonement*. "My God, my God, why hast thou forsaken me?" They are startling and mysterious words. They are words of agony and separation. Yet we must thank God for that separation, for it proves to us that atonement was real. How can we be sure our sins were actually placed upon Jesus Christ? We know because of the awful separation Christ experienced. Only sin could so separate the Father and the Son. Only your sins and mine could make such a division necessary. The horrible exclamation of Jesus is a wonderful confirmation for us that atonement is real.

Jesus was, and is, God—as much God as the Father Himself. Still, He was human, and as a human He said, "I thirst." He could not have saved us without being human. The sins of mankind were human sins. As such they demanded a human sacrifice, or a human substitute. Jesus became Man so that He could become our Substitute. That is why we call His fifth statement from the cross the *Affirmation of Substitution*. He became our Substitute.

As a Man, Jesus learned the reality of suffering. He learned what it meant to be lied about. He discovered how it felt to be betrayed. He learned the pressures of temptation and overcame them. He experienced the darkness of grief and survived it. He has lived where we live. He has walked where we walk. He became our Substitute, not only to provide a sacrifice for our sins but also to provide a sympathetic heart for our times of need. No one can more sympathetically identify with our times of grief, and our times of joy, than Jesus. He has experienced what we have experienced.

"It is finished." This sixth saying is the triumphant climax of Calvary. It is the *Affirmation of Exultation*. These words affirm for us the truth that the means and way of salvation are complete. There will never be another Savior, nor need for one. There will never be another Lamb, nor need for one. The work has been finished. We know this to be true by Jesus' own affirmation.

Finally, we have the *Affirmation of Glorification*. "Father, into thy hands I commend my spirit." When this life is over, there is another. When our existence in these frail bodies has ceased, another and better existence awaits us. When Jesus had suffered all that any man could suffer, He affirmed for us the glory that is to come by placing Himself in the hands of His Father for eternity. The end of life on earth should not be a time of fear. It was not for our Lord. We should view it, instead, as a time of entering into rest. It is a time when we, weary from the toils of life and

93

no longer able to tend to our own needs, lean back on the loving hands of our heavenly Father. Glory awaits us. Christ has affirmed it.

SEVEN SIGNIFICANT WORDS

We have looked at the sayings from the cross. We have studied them individually. We have looked at them as affirming great truths. Still, there is one other sense in which we should view those sayings. Let us condense them into seven significant words, words that capture for our hearts and imaginations the message of the cross.

The first word is *forgiveness*. Jesus asked His Father to forgive the sinners who had nailed Him to the cross. The cross is forgiveness for us.

The second word is *companionship*. The thief who died by Jesus' side has become His companion for eternity. The cross means an eternal companionship between the believer and Jesus Christ.

The third word is *relationship*. Jesus recognized the importance of His relationship with His mother and with John. He emphasized the importance of earthly relationships by asking God to care for His mother. There will be a new type of relationship when we enter heaven. This will be a personal and intimate relationship with the God of the universe and with His Son.

The fourth word is *forsakenness*. Again, the emphasis is upon the supreme sacrifice which Jesus willingly made on our behalf. He was totally forsaken by God and man.

The fifth word is *mortality*. Jesus suffered as a human being. All humans suffer. Christ suffered for us and with us so that some day we could be delivered from all suffering.

The sixth word is *accomplishment*. Jesus has accomplished all that God requires. There is nothing else to be added to our salvation. It is complete. It has been accomplished. The work of Christ is sufficient, by itself, for our everlasting salvation.

The seventh word is *security*. How beautiful it is to know that the Lord can forgive, cleanse, and forget! Our sins are remembered against us no more. We are secure in Him. When we come to the cross, when we know Him, we have eternal life.

Seven sayings, seven affirmations, seven meaningful words. When next you receive the Lord's Supper, whether in a formal church service or in an informal gathering of believers, remember these statements of Christ and their importance to you. If it is the purpose of the Lord's Supper to bring us to a remembrance of what was accomplished by the broken body and shed blood of Christ, then the reality of that ordinance is enhanced by our calling to mind the seven things Jesus said during His hours on the cross.

8
Himself He Cannot Save

And it was the third hour, and they crucified him. And the superscription of his accusation was written over, THE KING OF THE JEWS. And with him they crucify two thieves; the one on his right hand, and the other on his left. And the scripture was fulfilled, which saith, And he was numbered with the transgressors. And they that passed by railed on him, wagging their heads, and saying, Ah, thou that destroyest the temple, and buildest it in three days, Save thyself, and come down from the cross. Likewise also the chief priests mocking said among themselves with the scribes, He saved others; himself he cannot save (Mark 15:25–31).

WHAT'S IN A NAME?

Our enemies often know more about us than our friends do. Often an accusation or observation an enemy makes contains the seed of a great and living truth. We call ourselves Christians. The disciples were called Christians first in Antioch. It was not a

97

name they chose for themselves. For instance, the name *Christian* was given to the believers of Antioch by unbelievers. Yet the name means Christ-like. There can be no better description of one who is tuly trusting in Jesus.

A more modern example of this trend can be seen in the term *Methodist*, as in the denomination by that name. The name *Methodist* was originally used in derision. People mocked John Wesley and his followers because of their methodical approach to religion. Wesley kept a journal of the events of each day. He rose each morning at a certain hour, followed a schedule throughout the day, and went to bed at a certain hour. There was a method in all that he did. He was a method-ist.

Sometimes when our enemies brand us, the brand becomes a badge or symbol of truth. When Jesus was tried and crucified He was surrounded by the chief leaders of the Jewish religion, the top preachers, scribes, intellectuals, and doctors. These men had opposed His ministry from its beginning. As He hung on the cross they mocked Him, and said, "He saved others; himself he cannot save." Their words contained more truth than even they understood.

WHY?

This accusation is a conundrum. A conundrum is a riddle or mystery whose solution is, or involves, a pun or paradox. Christ's situation was certainly a mysterious paradox. He could save others, but in doing so He could not save Himself. On the other hand, He *could* have saved Himself, but if He were to do so He would not have been able to save others. The men who accused Jesus did not understand the cross. If they had understood that Jesus was the Sacrifice for the sins of mankind, that knowledge would probably have led them to accept Him. They opposed Him for selfish and political reasons. They did not realize that He was Messiah.

There was, however, one thing that these men knew: Jesus saved others. They understood clearly that over on the other side of the Mount of Olives from where they stood was the home of Lazarus of Bethany. Lazarus was a great friend of Jesus. Some days earlier he had become ill and died. After Lazarus had been dead for four days, Jesus brought him back to life. Some of Christ's accusers may have attended the wake, eaten at the banquet, and stood at the tomb when it was sealed. They knew beyond doubt that Lazarus was dead. After the funeral crowds left Jesus came. After death left, life came and said, "Lazarus! Come forth!" and Lazarus came out of the grave. The people loosed him from his burial clothes and set him free. Jesus' accusers knew this was true, because the man who had been buried probably marched through the streets saying, "Jesus has raised me from the dead." You would think they would love Jesus because of this miracle. But they did not. Neither did they love Lazarus. They wanted to kill Jesus because of the miracle He had performed, and Lazarus because he was living proof of that miracle.

Jesus' accusers also knew that down by the city of Jericho, where they went in summer and winter for therapeutic baths, down where they went to enjoy the warm climate, in that city two thousand five hundred feet below Jerusalem, was a man born blind. His name was Bartimaeus. He had spent his entire life sitting by the roadside begging for alms, until the day Jesus came and gave him his sight. This man went about telling everyone that Jesus, the Son of David, had healed him and had ushered him out of a world of darkness into the light of day.

The accusers had to confess that He had certainly saved others, but herein was the conundrum—He did not use the same power to save Himself. These men understood that on two occasions Jesus had used just a few loaves of bread and a few fish to feed multitudes of people. They had heard all about that.

They knew of ten lepers who had been cleansed by the words of Jesus.

They knew about a man who had been born crippled, yet was made whole by this Man who was now hanging on a cross before them. They knew that for years He had gone about healing others. There was hardly anyone in Jerusalem or in the surrounding towns who did not personally know someone who had seen Jesus' healing power. But these intellectuals and religious leaders were faced with a seemingly fathomless mystery: Jesus had saved countless others; why would He not, could He not save Himself?

THE GREAT PARADOX

In their mocking, these men had stumbled onto one of the great truths of all time. If Christ had saved

Himself, He could not have saved others. This is not a truth easily grasped. It must be allowed to sink deep within the heart before it can have meaning. If Christ had saved Himself, He could not have saved the world. It was only because He refused to save Himself that He could offer salvation to you and me, to the human race. These men, with unbelieving hearts, could not understand this. It is a foundational truth for every Christian, but it was beyond their ability to conceive. If Jesus had done as they suggested and come down from the cross, you and I would go to hell. We would have no Savior. We would have no Redeemer. We would have no Healer. We would have no Master. We would have no Lord. We would have no salvation. This is the great paradox of Christianity.

If He had saved Himself, we would be lost. But because He was willing to lose Himself, we can be saved. No heathen god can stand in the light of such self-sacrifice. The gods of the heathen are angry gods. They are gods of evil, selfish gods. The traditions of the heathens tell us of no god willing to die so that people might have life. Jesus, and only Jesus, would do such a thing.

He left all that was rightfully His, all that heaven could offer, and came to earth on our behalf. He lost, as it were, all the majesty of His heavenly position. He lost the splendor of a throne for the humility of a carpenter's shop. He lost the adoration of angels and accepted, instead, the derision of men. He lost the dignity of His royal position and accepted the shame of public execution.

He loved the world so much, He loved you and me so much, that He was willing to face the most ignominious of deaths that the world could offer, crucifixion on a Roman cross. It was His choice. No one, not even His Father, forced Him to do it. He chose to become a spectacle for the world to see. He died on a cross, deliberately and willfully. It was His choice. He had everything and gave it up so that He might save us. Had He for even a moment grasped at His previous possessions, we would have been lost. Had He even once thought more of Himself than of us, there would have been no salvation. Had He saved Himself, we would have been lost. Instead He gave up all that He had so that we could be saved.

DELEGATION OF RESPONSIBILITY

After His resurrection, Jesus assembled His disciples and said to them, ". . . Go ye into all the world, and preach the gospel to every creature" (Mark 16:15). He could just as well have said, "Go to everyone in your generation and tell them the gospel of salvation." He made reaching the world a primary objective of New Testament believers. Over four billion people are living at the same time as we. God's Holy Spirit has given us a desire to see them saved. We want them to know the same joy of salvation we have experienced. But how can we hope to tell them all? What can we do to reach them?

God, in His own sovereign fashion, has chosen to delegate the responsibility of reaching the world to us. We are His hands, His feet, His mouth, and His

ears. God has no other hands, feet, mouth, eyes, or
ears in this present age except yours and mine. He
has told us to preach the gospel to the world. We
must conclude, then, that He expects us to do this,
and surely He would not commission us to do a task
He knows is impossible. God wants us to reach our
generation with the gospel. The words of those who
accused Jesus give us an important key to accom-
plishing that goal.

MESSAGE AND MANNER

I mentioned earlier that Christians were first called
by that name in Antioch. It was a title given them by
unbelievers. Even the lost could recognize in Christians a quality that set them apart from others. They
were like Christ. If we are ever to accomplish the
task of reaching our generation for Christ, we must
understand from the beginning that the task rests
upon two important elements: our message and our
manner of life. The message alone is not enough. If
we present the message of salvation to others while
displaying with our lives an attitude of defeat, sorrow,
bitterness, hatred, jealousy, and hyprocrisy, it is not
likely that our message will be warmly received.
When the message we present and our manner of life
are not consistent, we cannot expect the message to
be taken seriously.

On the other hand, the manner of life alone is not
enough. If we lead a life of love and joy and peace and
contentment, but refuse to share the source of these
virtues with others, we will fail in our mission.

Successful evangelism, successful completion of the great commission, demands a proper balance between the message of the gospel and the manner of life of the believer. The observation of those who mocked Jesus can give us valuable insight into these two areas.

First consider the message. "He saved others," the mockers said. This is the message of the gospel. It is the message of the Lord's Supper: Jesus saves. He allowed His body to be broken and His blood to be shed in order to pay for the sins of a world that deserves to go to hell. He paid the penalty for sin and satisfied the demands of God's righteousness. He became the Mediator between God and man. He is the Lamb of God who takes away the sins of the world. All who believe in Him and receive Him as Savior can have eternal life. True, if we repeat the message loud enough and frequently enough there will be those who, in spite of our inconsistent manner of life, will receive Christ and be saved. The message is a powerful one, but its effectiveness depends, in part, on the manner of life of those who present it. A great portion of these chapters has dealt with the message itself. Most of us are familar with it, so we will devote no further time to it here.

Let us turn to the manner of life of the believer, and its importance in carrying out the Great Commission. The mocking leaders of the religious crowd said, "Himself He cannot save." This great truth should be the ultimate example for all who would effectively carry out the great commission. Jesus was unwilling to save Himself. Instead, He laid down

His life to save others. Those who would effectively reach others with the gospel of Jesus Christ must be willing to say, "Myself I cannot save." If we are to fulfill the great commission we must be willing to lay down everything, just as Jesus did. We must be willing to give up ourselves for the sake of others.

Men always look for a bargain. We live in the day of discounts. Discount department stores flourish. Housewives collect discount coupons with zeal. The merchant who can offer the lowest price is generally the one who can win the most business. Sadly, Christians have the same attitude toward evangelism.

We want to save the world, but we want to save it with a tip, like the tip we leave for a waitress. We are content to drop our tip on God's table and be gone on our way. That sort of attitude will not save the world. Most of us would like to see the world saved, but only if it can be done in a way that will not inconvenience us, a way that will not hurt us, a way that will not make demands on our time or our pocketbooks. But if we are to save the world, we must do it in the manner that Jesus did. That does not mean, of course, that every Christian must suffer a Roman execution. I do not mean to suggest that every believer should shed his own blood, though each of us should certainly be willing to do that if God demands it. I am saying that saving the world is not possible without blood, sweat, and tears.

DISCIPLESHIP

Jesus said, ". . . If any man will come after me, let

him deny himself, and take up his cross, and follow me" (Matt. 16:24). Do we really wish to go after Jesus? Do we wish to be his disciples? Such discipleship does not come cheaply. Christ's formula for discipleship is simple, yet costly to initiate. His three steps, His three laws, His formula for discipleship is this: Deny yourself, take up your cross, follow Me.

If we intend to have a lifestyle that gives credibility to our message, we must be disciples of Christ in the truest sense. From the beginning of the church there have been those who have tried to live the life in public while following their own whims in private. That approach does not work. The church will always have Ananias and Sapphira, who tried to put on a public display of Christianity while hiding a heart of deceit; even a lost world can see through that brand of religion. The manner of life, the lifestyle, which gives a genuine ring to the message of the gospel is one that can only be ours when we know Christ in His fullness.

If we try to act like Christ without knowing the fullness of His power in our lives, the world will see us merely as actors. The manner of life that reinforces the message of the gospel is not something we can develop by our own efforts. It is a work of the Holy Spirit. It is a manifestation of the life of Christ in us. It is a display of the union we spoke of in earlier chapters. The manner of life that tells the world our message is true is the manner of life that declares, in a way that words cannot, that we are united with Christ. That manner of life is real discipleship, which only comes when we deny ourselves, take up our cross, and follow Christ.

DENIAL

How many people do you know who are willing to deny themselves to save the world? We are speaking of immortal souls, of the eternal destiny of men and women. Do you know many who deny themselves for that cause? The principle of denying ourselves is a great equalizer. The rich man, the talented man, the man with much wealth or fame, may be called upon to deny a great deal. The poor man, the plain man, the simple man, may be called upon to deny himself of a relatively small amount. But Jesus does not measure that denial in terms of how much we have given up. He simply said, "Deny yourself."

He did not ask us to deny a portion of ourselves. He did not ask us to give up a little of what we have. He has asked us to deny ourselves in the same way that He denied Himself. He denied Himself the privilege of heaven's throne and the opportunity for regal splendor on earth in order to save the world. He did not give up some. He did not give up most. He gave up *all*. There are many areas in which we, as believers, can and should deny ourselves. The goal is not, however, to see who can give up the most. The goal is not to make ourselves feel good by constantly reminding ourselves of how much we have given up for Christ. The goal is to totally lay aside all of our resources, our abilities, our ambitions, even our families, in order to know Christ in the fullest sense. When we have known Him and walked with Him, then we will be able to tell others about Him, and more effectively reach our world for Christ.

The area of finance is often a difficult one to discuss. Frankly, many of the means we employ to spread the message of Christ are very expensive. Christian broadcasting requires a great deal of money. Operating even the simplest local church takes money. Sending missionaries to foreign lands requires considerable sums of money. I do not believe this is accidental. A man's attitude toward money tells us a great deal about his attitude toward God.

It is a true principle that when men and money come together one generally controls the other. A man who controls his money can keep it or spend it. He can give it to a worthy cause, invest it, or spend it to meet his daily needs. A man who, on the other hand, is controlled by his money is always trying to get more. He looks at financial decisions from the standpoint of personal gain and personal loss. Before he can give to a worthy cause, he must be assured that his gift is tax deductible. He often gives not so much to help the recipient as to soothe his own conscience. For him, giving is a means to an end, a way to gain favor with others or to soothe his own conscience and enhance his self-image. If he loses money through a bad investment, he grieves over the loss, never stopping to praise God for the lessons he may have learned through such an experience. In short, his money owns him to a larger extent than he owns it.

Whether he wishes to admit it or not, money, not God, is his master.

I am not suggesting that God endorses an irresponsible attitude toward money. He does not. He expects us to be faithful stewards of the financial resources He has given us. This is the key: They are resources *He* has given us. If we inherited them, they came to us from another and not from ourselves. If we received them as wages for labor, we should realize that we were only able to perform that labor because God graciously provided us with the ability to work and the opportunity to hold a job. In either case, we have the financial resources we enjoy only because God has allowed us to have them. In a real sense they are not ours at all. They are His, placed temporarily at our disposal.

To deny ourselves in the area of money means that we are willing to regard our entire income as a resource placed at our disposal by God. It is not ours. It is His. If He chooses to increase it, we praise Him. If he chooses to take it away, we praise Him still. If He tells us to give to a local church, we give. If He tells us to meet the needs of others, we meet those needs. To deny ourselves means that we are not constantly grasping for money, not constantly scheming for gain, not constantly planning bigger and better ways to get more.

Denying ourselves means that we are responsible for what God has given us but also willing to part with every dime if He should direct us to do so. I believe that God designed money as a type of spiritual barometer. One of the easiest ways to detect whether or not a person has truly denied himself is to observe his attitude toward money. If he is bound by money and controlled by it, it is not likely that he has truly denied himself in order to seek Christ. When preachers and churches and Christ-honoring ministries are constantly forced to beg for money, it is a pretty good indication that many who have accepted Christ have not denied themselves in order to follow Him.

God has promised that if we give, it shall be given to us, pressed down, shaken together, and running over. This is a guarantee from the Lord, just as much as His guarantee of salvation. Those who give up themselves for the Lord do not lose. God returns blessings to them until their lives overflow. Still, most Christians are so controlled by money that they cannot turn loose of it. The need, however, is not for Christians to give up their money. The need is for Christians to deny themselves. If more believers would truly deny themselves in order to seek Christ, the financial difficulties of most ministries would cease. When those believers have truly denied themselves, money would no longer control them. Money would no longer fill such an important position in their lives, and they would be more willing to give. God would bless their giving with prosperity, and they would be willing and able to give again.

There is a definite cycle to giving. We give ourselves to God. He leads us to give our finances. As we give, He gives to us again. Then we are able to give a second time, renewing the cycle. It goes on endlessly.

Unfortunately, this cycle is rarely observed in today's church. Since few believers have truly denied themselves, they are still caught up in and controlled by the desire for money. They do not give, and God does not bless. The result is that the message is not presented to those who have never heard it. Denying ourselves does not mean giving of our finances. It is certainly possible to give for the wrong reasons. However, it is not possible for a person who has truly denied himself and begun to see Christ to have a selfish and grasping attitude toward his personal finances.

We do not become a better disciple by giving money, but our attitude toward giving money can certainly reveal whether or not we are a true disciple, whether or not we have denied ourselves to follow Christ.

Jesus knew that if He were to save the world, He could not save Himself. He had to give Himself for others. He expects no less of us. In a practical sense He expects us to place ourselves totally at His disposal, to hold back nothing, to totally deny ourselves. Our financial affairs are probably the most visible area through which we can discern whether we have totally given ourselves to God.

Make a quick inventory of your personal belongings. Many who are reading these pages own their homes. But is that home really yours? Many would reply that it is more the property of the mortgage company than it is theirs. In many cases this is true, but it is not our principal concern. Even if you hold a clear the title on your home, is it really yours? Do you regard your home as your personal property, or do you recognize it as God's property placed temporarily in your care?

What about that car you spent the past Saturday afternoon washing and waxing so carefully? Is it truly your property? Consider the television set, the stereo, the furniture, the clothes, the appliances, and the other personal items in your home. Are they really yours? Many of us, at one time or another, have experienced a time of dedication. It may have been at the altar of our church. Perhaps it was while listening to a radio or television speaker. We may have experienced this time of dedication during our personal Bible reading or devotion time. In such a moment of dedication we may have presented ourselves totally to God. Certainly our intentions were good, but was the presentation real?

Using our finances as a barometer, let us consider how real that dedication was. Consider a typical man's wallet. If we were to open it and examine the contents we might find some money, several credit cards, a driver's license, a Social Security card, membership cards to various organizations, pictures of family and friends, and other similar items. If we lay the wallet on the table, it stands to reason that we have also laid all the contents of the wallet on the table. It is not necessary for us to remove the contents from the wallet and spread them on the table top. By simply placing the wallet on the table, we have placed its contents there as well. If we put the wallet in a box, seal the box, and mail it to a friend, we have mailed the wallet and all of its contents to that person.

Where the wallet goes, the contents go. If we can see ourselves and our lives as that wallet, then the illustration becomes meaningful.

Our lives contain our personal possessions, our occupation and all that concerns it, our ambitions, our plans, our dreams, our goals, our children, our relatives, our husbands or wives. Where our lives go, all the things that make up our lives must go as well. Many Christians are content to give God the wallet, but only after they have emptied it of all its contents. They are willing to give God something abstract, their life. They are not willing, however, to give God something concrete, the things that make up their lives.

When we dedicated our life to Christ, did we give Him the things that make up our life? Can we honestly say that our monthly income is God's? Is our home God's? Is our car God's? Are our personal belongings God's? What about our job? Have we given it to God? Are we willing to part with it if God should lead us to do so? Would we be willing to give up our careers, if God so required, in order to take the gospel to those who have never heard? Of course, God does not require everyone to become a missionary or a preacher or an evangelist. He only requires that we be willing to do so if He asks. What about our ambitions? Have we truly given our plans and dreams and goals to God? Has there ever been a time when we have told Him we would be willing to lay aside all that we have ever wanted to do and all we have ever wanted to be in order to serve Him? That is the essence of denying ourselves. It is being willing to put aside everything,

113

if God asks. And everything includes our family, friends, and loved ones.

How many of us, who hope our children will become doctors or lawyers, would be willing to give them to God so that they might become missionaries or preachers or teachers of the gospel? Have we turned our husbands and our wives and our children and our loved ones over to Christ for His use? Have we so totally denied ourselves that God is free to take and use everything that we have?

The first step toward effective discipleship is to deny ourselves. To deny ourselves is to deny all claim on everything and everyone. To deny ourselves is to turn our lives over to God. To deny ourselves is to allow Him to do whatever He wants, whenever He wants, with anything and everything that makes up our lives. Ourselves we cannot save. If we try to tell the world of the gospel of Christ while clinging selfishly to our financial resources, our occupational interests, our personal ambitions, and our relationships with others, our manner of life may weaken our message. If we would save the world, we cannot save ourselves. That means denying everything that we have in order to reach others. Jesus did this, and invites us to do the same.

TAKING UP THE CROSS

The second step on the road to discipleship is to take up our cross. It seems like a simple thing to take up our cross. We may put it on a chain and wear it around our neck. We may put it on top of the steeple of our church, or hang it on the wall in our home. But that cross is not our cross. That is Jesus' cross. Our cross is not silver or gold. It is not ornamental. It is a heavy cross, a burdensome cross, a cross to be despised. The work that Jesus did on the cross has been completed. He died there and carried away forever the curse of sin. We may use the symbol of the cross to remind us of what He has done for us, but we should not mistake that symbol for our own cross.

Many are eager to take up Jesus' cross. They enjoy basking in the truth that their sins are forgiven. They enjoy standing in the shade of Jesus' cross and leaning back on the truth that He has completed the requirements for our salvation. There is nothing wrong with this, unless we become so enamored with Jesus' cross that we neglect to take up our own. Bearing our cross is a daily matter. It is a matter of living and giving and working for the Master.

We have already said that discipleship does not come cheaply. Neither does crucifixion come painlessly. In Roman times it was customary to require a condemned criminal to carry his own cross to the place of execution. Jesus was required to carry His own cross until He became so weak from the physical abuse He had experienced that He could no longer bear the load. Bearing one's cross became an expression, which meant being condemned to death.

When Jesus said we should take up our cross, He was using the expression of His time, which meant that we should be willing to die. When He said that His disciples would be required to take up their crosses, those who were listening did not misunder-

115

stand. They did not picture someone simply picking up a wooden cross and moving it from one location to another. They clearly understood that Jesus was speaking of death.

This does not, of course, mean that in order to become a disciple of Jesus Christ we must be killed. Quite the contrary, He expects us to live for Him on a daily basis. Still, there is death. When we spoke of Saul of Tarsus in an earlier chapter, we said that he died on the road to Damascus. All that Saul had been passed away. From that day forward there was a new man, a man born again by the grace of God. He was a new creature; the old had died. The new man, Paul, later wrote, "I am crucified with Christ: nevertheless I live; yet not I, but Christ liveth in me: and the life which I now live in the flesh I live by the faith of the Son of God, who loved me, and gave himself for me" (Gal. 2:20). Paul was recognizing the fact that when Jesus died, Paul died with Him. We should all recognize this as truth.

When we accept Christ we accept His death as our own. Our old man is passed away. A new man is born. The Cruxifixion happened once, and only once. It cannot and will not be repeated. Still, there is a sense in which we must take up our cross daily. We must be sentenced to death daily. Those parts of us which are still very much like the world must die daily. If we are to reach the world for Christ we must, on a daily basis, allow God to crucify those things which link us to the old life.

Do you recall the three crosses we spoke of earlier?

Do you recall that Paul said he had been crucified to the world and the world crucified to him? That concept applies here as well. Our cross is the cross upon which those things which link us to our old way of life are to be nailed. Sometimes it can be painful. Sometimes we will see things that we once enjoyed, and are not quite ready to give up, being nailed to the cross. Sometimes the ambitions, hopes, ideas, and financial resources which we gave to God will be openly nailed to the cross. Often it is unpleasant, but it is God's way. And God's way is always best.

There is another sense in which it can be painful. Bearing the cross of Jesus may mean that we will also experience the ridicule He experienced. Jesus was laughed at; we may be laughed at. Jesus was mocked; we may be mocked. The people with whom we work at the shop or office may call us preacher. They may turn up their noses at us and say we are prudish or puritanic. They may ridicule us for refusing to engage in sin. They may abuse us. They may give us a taste of what Jesus experienced on our behalf. But Jesus experienced it and survived. If we depend upon Him for strength we will be able to survive it as well. And when we do, people will see in our manner of life a testimony that proves to them the reality of the message we preach.

If we buckle under their ridicule, they may conclude that our message is just as shaky as we are. It is important for us to bear our cross on a daily basis, without complaint, so that others might be brought to Christ by our testimony. If we would save the world, we cannot save ourselves. It we would reach others for Christ, if we would be His disciple, we must be willing to bear our own cross daily.

FAITHFUL FOLLOWERS

Finally, if we would be effective disciples, we must follow Jesus. We must be willing to go where He tells us to, and do what He tells us to. If we have not denied ourselves, when He calls we may be too busy with our own affairs to follow. Therefore we must deny ourselves, lay our own affairs aside. If we are not willing to take up our cross, when He calls we may feel that the task is too difficult. We may not feel that we can complete it. It is important that we pick up our cross, and bear whatever pain is necessary to reach others. When we have put aside our own affairs and have shown ourselves ready and willing to suffer for Christ, He will lead. When He leads, we will be able to follow. We will not be bound by the affairs of the world or discouraged by the difficulty of the task.

When we follow Him, there will be a genuine ring to our life. Our message will not be weakened by personal hypocrisy. The combination of the message of the gospel and the pure and honest life of discipleship will make it possible for us to save those around us.

To the best of my knowledge, Christians who would deny themselves and take up their crosses to follow Christ are in the minority. God has given us three steps to discipleship, but we have not obeyed. We say, "Lord, save the world," but He will not do it. He has chosen to work through *us*, and He cannot work through us until we are willing to obey Him, until we are willing to give up ourselves for others.

The church of our generation has saved itself and lost the world. The multitudes no longer attend the churches; we have lost them. There was a time when almost everyone went to church. That time is no more. Why did we lose them? Because we saved ourselves. Sinners know that many of the great denominations have large sums of money and great resources in Wall Street. They see the wealth of these great religious organizations and read of their intricate plans to avoid taxation, and conclude that Christians are more concerned with themselves than with the lost. They conclude, and too often are correct, that the church is out to save itself, not the world. We have heard many Christian brothers say they are saving for a rainy day. Such an idea is certainly not from God, for He has promised to supply our every need every day. Again, I am not suggesting that Christians become irresponsible with their money, only that they realize God is their source of supply.

It is not right for religious leaders and denominations to build up millions of dollars in assets while the world is going to hell. It is time for Christians to be willing to lose themselves in order to save the world.

As Jesus hung on the cross, the religious leaders of His day stood by and mocked. They said, "He saved others; Himself He cannot save." They were right. He had saved others. They were also right in saying

He could not save Himself. He could not, not if He expected to save the world. Could those who observe our lives say the same of us? Or would they conclude that we have saved ourselves and lost the world?

9
The Suffering Savior

There is nothing in Christendom so moving as the Crucifixion. Christ's crucifixion is memorialized for us through Holy Communion, possibly the most stirring exercise of Christian worship. We are always glad for Communion day, when we can come before the Lord and remember the body that was broken for us and the blood that was shed for us. As we receive Communion, it is not unusual for us to recall the suffering Jesus experienced. We will speak of that suffering in this chapter. However, we seldom stop to think that the Trinity was involved at Calvary. We understand that Christ was there, but we sometimes overlook the fact that the Father and the Holy Spirit were there also.

In John 3:16 we read, "For God so loved the world, that he gave his only begotten Son, that whosoever believeth in him should not perish, but have everlasting life." The purpose of Calvary is everlasting life. God loved the world, and loves it still. He loves each and every man and woman and boy and girl in it. Because of that love, He desires for all of us to share in eternal life with Him. The only way this can happen is through Jesus Christ. God gave us His Son so

121

that we can have eternal life. Eternal life, or everlasting life, is the central theme and sole purpose for Calvary.

I am grateful to have had the opportunity to personally climb Mount Calvary. The first time I stood on the summit of Golgotha, it seemed that in my spirit I could almost see unfolding before me the most agonizing drama of all time. There is only one smooth route to the top of Calvary, only one way you can reach the summit without encountering high ledges or steep cliffs. That smooth route is most certainly the same one that would have been taken two thousand years ago. As I walked up that hill, slowly, step by step, a wonderful feeling swept over me. It brought to mind the scene that transpired on that mountain those many years ago. It recalled the passion, not only of Jesus, but of the entire Trinity. They were all involved. It was a display of love to the total human race, all men of all places, and it purchased salvation for everyone who believes.

THE HEART THAT GRIEVES IS THE HEART THAT LOVES

The first Person of the Trinity, God the Father, was a principal Participant in the events of Calvary. The Father grieved over lost mankind. Scripture tells us the sin of man brought great grief to God the Father. We are even told that the Father once repented that He had made men. Man had gone so far in the wrong direction, and God was hurt so deeply by it, that God concluded it would have been better for the entire race if it had not been created. Yet the heart that grieves is the heart that loves. As we read John 3:16, we see that. The Father had such intense love and care and emotion for mankind that He was willing to go through the depths of sorrow, willing to give His own Son, in order to save the fallen race.

The Father was very much a part of the Crucifixion. He was there in His Son, listening to every word. When the Son looked up to Him and said, "Father, forgive them, for they know not what they do," He was close by saying, "I do. I have. I will." Jesus had taught His disciples that He and the Father were One. Because They were, and are, One, the Father was much involved in the suffering of Christ's passion. He was involved in the salvation of the human race. He was listening carefully to every word. He was watching every event intently. When the ultimate sacrifice was offered by His Son, when Jesus laid down His life for men who had broken the laws of God and turned their backs upon His righteousness, God the Father received and accepted that sacrifice.

LOVE IS CAPABLE OF SUFFERING

Any being capable of love is also capable of suffering. God is love. Therefore He is certainly capable of suffering. Love and suffering are linked to love's object. Those whom we love the most have the greatest capacity to cause us suffering. If we are rejected or insulted by someone for whom we care very little, we will not suffer much over that rejection or insult. But if we are rejected or insulted by one whom we love deeply, that rejection or insult will cause deep pain. God loves us. He suffers when we do wrong, and He suffers when we suffer.

Traveling the world, I have had the opportunity of evangelizing and ministering in one hundred nations. In those nations I saw and studied heathen deities. Heathen gods are gods of anger and hate and revenge and punishment. In most cultures there is no god of love. When there is, it is generally a god of selfish physical love, not a god of divine love and divine sacrifice. The heathen countries know nothing of a god who suffers when people suffer and who is willing to endure that suffering to see people saved. We must go to Calvary to know that sort of God. God the Father was present, through His Son, experiencing all the pain and suffering of Calvary. The passion of the Son was also the passion of the Father.

We see then, that the love which made Calvary a reality was the love which involved God the Father in the events that took place there. In giving His Son, and loving those for whom His Son was given, God the Father had a part in Calvary.

THE HOLY SPIRIT AT CALVARY

The Holy Spirit was also involved in this most dramatic period of human history. When the Son of God, suspended on a cross between the heavens and the earth, was giving Himself to save mankind, the Holy Spirit was there. The Holy Spirit is mentioned for the first time in Scripture on the first page of the Bible, where it says that He moved upon the waters. He brought cosmos out of chaos. That has been His business ever since, seeking to bring beauty out of ungodliness, seeking to bring order out of disorder. But the most important work of the Holy Spirit is not the work of creation, it is the part He plays in the new creation.

It was the Father who gave the Son. It was the Son who gave His life, and it is the Spirit who draws us to salvation. Whatever our color or race, it is the Holy Spirit who works in our hearts, leading us to Calvary. The work Jesus accomplished on the cross is continued by the Holy Spirit. It is impossible for us to know Christ unless the Holy Spirit brings us to Him. In that sense, the Holy Spirit was very much part of Calvary. He is closely related to the process through which we receive salvation, for He draws us to the cross and brings us to repentance. He is the One who works in us, and when we have come to the Lord Jesus, He is the One who fills us and empowers us to share that message with others. He is the One who helps us to understand the Scriptures. He is the One who quickens our hearts and minds to spiritual truths.

We may wonder whether the Holy Spirit truly had a part in the work of Calvary. But if we understand that work at all, we must conclude that He did. For if He had no part in that work, then Calvary would not be alive in our own hearts. He is the One who has given us understanding of what Jesus did, and He is the One who has drawn us to accept Jesus as Savior.

THE PASSION OF THE SON

We come now to the One whom we understand as having a greater part in Calvary than any other member of the Godhead. He is, of course, our Lord Jesus Christ—the Son of God. The passion of the Son of God is so great the entire New Testament staggers under the weight of the agony of His sufferings. The New Testament begins with One who lived in sublime glory, seated upon a throne, with ten thousand times ten thousand heavenly creatures bowing and adoring Him, crying, "Holy, holy, holy, Lord God Almighty." From all that splendor He came to a simple manger in Bethlehem.

Jesus apparently led a relatively uneventful early life. We are told little about Him until shortly before His ministry began. Then He began going throughout Judea and Galilee, preaching, teaching, and healing the sick. Some thought He was a prophet. Others accepted Him as the Messiah. Many thought He would overthrow the Roman government and establish an earthly kingdom. His ministry came to a climax when one of His disciples betrayed Him and conspired with His enemies to have Him crucified. The intensity of the anguish which the Lord Jesus Christ experienced was so great that not even His closest friends could understand. His own mother, His own disciples and friends, could not comprehend the crimson curtain that fell across the final days of His ministry.

Some of His disciples wanted Him to remain in the area across the Jordan and escape possible death. Others wanted to make Him a King so that they would not be forced to watch Him die. They were unable to understand. They could not comprehend until later, after that veil that separated man and God had been torn and a new way opened up to the heart of the Father. They were unable to see the depth of His suffering until after His resurrection, until after He had given to them His Holy Spirit. Because Jesus was an infinite Being, we will not understand the extent of His suffering until we have been united with Him in heaven. We can, however, in looking back over the events of Calvary, reach a certain understanding of the passion of Christ.

SUFFERING AS GOD

Jesus suffered as only the divine can suffer. His love was infinite, so the pain of His broken heart was equally infinite. The depth of His companionship with His Father was beyond measure; therefore, the agony of His separation was beyond our comprehension. The rejection He felt, the loneliness He experienced, the sorrow He endured, were all greater than our finite minds can comprehend. As God He suffered more than any human being can ever suffer. As God He was the source of life, yet He suffered the pain of laying that life aside. As God He shared in all of heaven, yet suffered the humiliation of laying all of His heavenly inheritance aside in order to face death as a criminal. As God He suffered in a way that man cannot.

SUFFERING AS A MAN

But Jesus was also human, and He suffered as a Man. He endured anguish in all three areas of the human personality. The Bible teaches us that humans have spirits, souls, and bodies. Christ suffered in all of these. The spirit is that part of man which communicates with God. When Adam sinned, his spirit was rendered dead. His communication with God was effectively cut off. That communication can only be restored through the new birth. Jesus, not being a son of Adam, was not born spiritually dead. His Spirit was a divine Spirit, and was alive to God from the beginning. That line of communication was never broken until Calvary. Then the Spirit that had always known perfect fellowship with the Father was suddenly cast into darkness and loneliness. The Spirit that had never experienced the inherited death of Adam's seed suddenly came face to face with the death penalty for the sins of all the ages.

We cannot know the depth of the suffering Jesus experienced in the spiritual realm. We can only speculate. But surely His suffering in this area was great, for His Spirit was totally pure, and there was nothing pure at Calvary.

Christ also suffered in His soul. The soul is made up of mind, will, and emotions. It is the seat of our intellect. It is the dwelling place of our feelings. It is the residence of the will. As we recall the words Jesus spoke while on the cross, we realize that His mind was alert until the end. In the midst of all the pain, He refused the solution of gall and vinegar that might have deadened His mind and eased the agony. He chose to remain in control of His faculties. It would have been impossible for Him to have gone through all that Calvary represents, totally alert from beginning to end, without having suffered great mental anguish. His mind, His intellect, was fully involved in the pain of the cross. You will recall, as well, that He cried out with a loud voice. Surely His emotions were involved, too.

He also suffered the loss of His will. He totally surrendered His determination to God the Father. He said, "Not my will, but Thine be done." All of the soul of Christ was involved. He gave Himself fully, mind, will, and emotions. His Spirit suffered. His soul suffered.

The body is the part of man we can see. We cannot see the spirit, though we may observe the results of its activity. We cannot see the soul, though we may see evidence of its existence. We can, however, see the body. As we consider Calvary we cannot escape the terrible sight of the physical suffering of Christ, the suffering He experienced in His body. He was stripped and beaten. A crown of thorns was placed upon His head. His beard was plucked out. He was abused. He was nailed to a cross, pierced with a spear, and left hanging, exposed to the elements.

All of this He suffered on our behalf. The prophet Isaiah wrote that He was wounded for our transgressions. There are five basic types of flesh wounds known to medical science. They are the contusion or bruise, the laceration, the wound of penetration, the wound of perforation, and the wound of incision. Jesus suffered each of these types of wounds.

BRUISED FOR OUR INIQUITIES

Let us deal first with the contusion, or *bruise*. We

read in Isaiah 53:5 that Jesus was bruised for our iniquities. It is remarkable that seven hundred years before Christ there was a man of God who understood that One would come to save the world, and that He would be bruised for our sins. Verse 10 of this same chapter tells us that it pleased the Lord to bruise Him. In other words, God's love for us was so strong that He gladly allowed His Son to be bruised in order to save us.

A bruise, or a contusion, generally comes from a blunt instrument. That instrument may be a club or a clenched fist. We can understand, then, that Isaiah's prophecy was fulfilled in Matthew 26:67. For there we are told that the soldiers spat upon His face and buffeted Him. The word *buffet* means to strike savagely with a clenched fist. The Roman soldiers literally beat Jesus about the face with their fists until He was bruised beyond recognition. Prophetically speaking, Isaiah describes Him by saying that, ". . . his visage was so marred more than any man, and his form more than the sons of men" (Isa. 52:14). He was so severely bruised that He could no longer be recognized as a man. Much of this terrible bruising came when He was beaten, buffeted, by His Roman captors. It was a bruising that He suffered and accepted for us.

SCOURGING

The second type of wounds Jesus received were *lacerations*. We read in Matthew 27:26 that Pilate had Jesus scourged. Scourging is beating with a whip.

130

When we look back through the Word of God, we read the words of David, the sweet psalmist of Israel, in Psalm 129:1–3. "Many a time have they afflicted me from my youth, may Israel now say: Many a time have they afflicted me from my youth: yet they have not prevailed against me. The plowers plowed upon my back: they made their long furrows." More than a thousand years before Christ was born, writing prophetically, David spoke of the men who plowed furrows in the back of God's Holy One. Before Rome became a world power, before the dreaded Roman scourge became a common means of punishment, God had determined the form of punishment which Christ would bear for our sins.

The scourging was executed with a Roman cat-of-nine-tails, a whip with nine leather thongs. At the end of each thong was fastened a piece of metal, glass, bone, or stone, As the victim was beaten, these sharp barbs cut deep furrows into his back. The Romans prescribed thirty-nine lashes upon the back with this whip, a punishment that literally tore the flesh away from the ribs and vertebrae of its victim. When Jesus received such a scourging, when He was wounded for our transgressions, He was fulfilling the prophecies of Isaiah and David. This is one of the reasons why we can have confidence in the Bible and accept it as fact. This is one of many instances in which a prophetic statement was later fulfilled in minute detail. Deep furrows were cut into the back of Jesus Christ, just as prophecy suggested. That beating was suffered on our account, and the blood which flowed from those wounds was shed to save us.

THE "CROWN" OF THORNS

The third wounds Jesus suffered were *penetration* wounds. These were inflicted when a crown of thorns was placed upon His head. The type of thorn tree from which this crown was made still grows in Palestine. The thorns are long and sharp. Rather than receiving a diadem of gold, Christ was crowned with these piercing thorns. The soldiers placed the crown upon His head and pushed it down until rivulets of blood flowed over His face. They mocked Him and said, "This man says he is a king. Let's make him king." The crown they gave Him was a crown of mocking. However, in prophesying of the kingdom which we will share with the Lord Jesus, Isaiah wrote, "Instead of the thorn shall come up the fir tree, and instead of the brier shall come up the myrtle tree: and it shall be to the LORD for a name, for an everlasting sign that shall not be cut off" (Isa. 55:13).

When He establishes His kingdom, Christ will eliminate those thorns forever. In the kingdom of God's pleasure there will be no thorns. That thing which became a mockery will be eliminated forever.

THE WOUNDS OF PERFORATION

The fourth wounds Jesus suffered were *perforation* wounds. After He had been brutally scourged, He was paraded through the streets of Jerusalem and led to the summit of Golgotha. There He lay on a wooden cross, and Roman soldiers drove heavy spikes through His hands and feet. They perforated the body of God's perfect man, nailing Him to the cross.

The cross was then erected for all to see. Christ was lifted up as a public spectacle.

Jesus said, "And as Moses lifted up the serpent in the wilderness, even so must the Son of man be lifted up: That whosoever believeth in him should not perish, but have eternal life" (John 3:14,15). In John 12:32,33 we read, "And I, if I be lifted up from the earth, will draw all men unto me." This He said, signifying by what death He would die. When Jesus spoke of being lifted up, He spoke of being lifted up on the cross of crucifixion. John understood this, and we must assume that many others who heard Jesus speak understood as well. He told Nicodemus that it was necessary for Him to be lifted up, or crucified, so that anyone believing in Him would not perish but would have eternal life. He also said that if He were lifted up He would draw men unto Himself.

The wounds of perforation, caused by the Roman spikes as they tore through the flesh of Christ, were a necessary part of God's plan to bring eternal life to mankind. He received those wounds so that we, by believing in Him, could have eternal life. Ever since receiving those wounds, He has been drawing men to Himself so that they might enjoy the eternal life He gives.

THE WOUND OF INCISION

The final wound Jesus received was an *incision*. We read of it in John 19:33,34. One of the soldiers took a spear and drove it deep into His side, just underneath the rib cage. His side was cut open, His heart was pierced, and all the organs and tissues surrounding the heart were opened. The blood that was to provide the salvation of the world poured from that incision and spilled on the ground. It was, as Judas Iscariot described it, the innocent blood. It was blood that was tainted neither by the inherited sin of Adam nor by individual sins.

Jesus was the Son of God and had received His sinless nature from His heavenly Father. He had lived a perfect life and knew no personal sin. His blood was truly innocent blood. More than that, it was *the* innocent blood.

Though we sing songs of Calvary and of the cross, we should understand that Calvary was a horrible event. Its participants knew nothing of the beauty sometimes attributed to it. It was a place of suffering and gory death. It was a place so gruesome that not even the light of the sun shone there for several hours. In the midst of it all was Christ. He was bruised. The Roman soldiers had beaten Him with their fists and abused Him. His body was covered with lacerations. The cat-of-nine-tails had cut deep furrows through His flesh until the skin surrounding His open wounds hung like bloody ribbons. Penetration wounds covered His head where the Roman soldiers had placed a mocking crown of thorns and had beaten it down into His skin with a reed. His hands and feet were scarred and perforated with large spikes. In His side was a yawning incision from which poured an eternal river of life-giving blood.

His heavenly Father was there, giving up His Son, yet unable to look upon Him because of the sin which

He bore. The Holy Spirit was there, drawing the attention of all men from eternity past until eternity future to the events that were transpiring. But most prominent in this scene of passion was Christ Himself.

Cruelty such as Jesus suffered seems beyond our comprehension. We may find it hard to imagine humans being so cruel to one another. Yet we must recall that man, without the indwelling Spirit of God, is capable of the grossest forms of evil. From the time that Cain lifted his hand to kill his brother, man has been hurting his fellow man. In addition to the suffering that we inflict upon ourselves, our world is filled with the suffering of disease and heartbreak. This is precisely why Jesus died. This is the reason He suffered. When He was wounded, He bore in His body our suffering for all eternity.

YOU CAN BE HEALED

I have come to know, in a small way, why He suffered as he did. Some years ago I had tuberculosis. The disease advanced quickly until I was given only hours to live. I had suffered with tubercular fever for six months. The doctors had done everything they could to eliminate it, but the disease persisted. I learned what it was like to heave and to cough up blood from my lungs. I could see no purpose in my suffering, and I began to wonder if God had deserted me. But He had not, and in answer to prayer I was healed. Since then God has allowed me to lead hundreds of people to be healed of tuberculosis.

Around the world I have shared the witness and testimony of God's healing in my life, and others have received healing through that testimony. When I lived in Hong Kong, where tuberculosis is a common disease, I visited a tubercular hospital, where I gave patients the testimony of my healing. My story was printed in Chinese and distributed. Several months later, in the church where I was pastor, we conducted a baptismal service exclusively for those people who were former patients at the tubercular hospital, people in whom the disease had been checked and healed by the power of God. We baptized twenty-three in one day.

If I had not gone through the valley of the shadow of death with that disease, I could not have shown others that healing was available to them. When I said to them, "You can be healed," they knew it was the truth. I had experienced it, and they could also.

Sometimes suffering is a good thing. It can be a blessing to others. Jesus suffered, and He wants us to know that He suffered every way that we can suffer. He was bruised, His body subjected to all types of wounds. We can take courage from the knowledge that He suffered these things and survived.

NO SUFFERING IN ETERNITY

In a greater sense, His suffering is not only an encouragement to us, it is the end of all suffering. Because Jesus suffered, there will be no suffering in eternity. If it had not been for His suffering, we would know the eternal suffering of hell. But because

He suffered, we do not have to. Whether we speak of heartache, disease, or the pain man inflicts upon man, we can be assured that it will all be eliminated in eternity.

Those who have had tuberculosis will receive new and healthy lungs. Those who have lived this life with the pain of arthritis will be relieved in heaven. The crippled will walk. The blind will see. The deaf will hear. The maimed will be perfectly formed. There will be no doctors, and no need of them, because our immortal bodies will be perfect. They will be free from disease and pain and hurt and suffering, all because Jesus suffered for us. We will be whole, but Jesus, throughout eternity, will have the signs in His palms and in His feet and in His side. He will be the only wounded and scarred person in eternity. We will forever be whole, because He will forever be scarred. We can know this is true because Thomas, when he looked upon the resurrected Lord, saw the evidence of His wounds. Those wounds are just as eternal as our salvation and healing. Of course, Christ will not be in pain. His pain ended when He arose victoriously from the grave. However, His body will bear the eternal reminders of the pain He suffered for us.

We cannot now see those wounds. Not even the most skilled artist can accurately portray them. The only evidence we now have of His wounding is His broken body and shed blood as presented to us in Holy Communion.

When we receive the bread, may we always think of the terrible manner in which that body was broken

137

and the terrible pain that body suffered. When we receive the cup, may we always be reminded of the wounds from which His precious blood flowed. When we receive the bread, may we hear Him saying, "This is my body which was broken for you. Because I have suffered, you will experience eternity without suffering." When we receive the cup, may we hear Him say, "This is the blood of the New Testament which was shed for many for the remission of sins. This blood was poured out so that you might have eternal life."

10
The Stigma of the Cross

Jesus Christ had the potential to become the greatest popular leader the world has ever seen. He fed the hungry. He took a small piece of bread, broke it, and fed a multitude. When everyone had eaten, there were still baskets full of bread left over. No other man has ever done that. He walked on the tempestuous waters of the sea. Neither Napoleon nor Charlemagne nor Julius Caesar nor Hitler nor any "hero" then or now has done that.

He touched the eyes of the blind, and they were instantly opened. He spoke to Lazarus, who had been dead for four days, and called him out of the grave. When He spoke, the dead came to life. No world ruler ever accomplished anything like that.

Jesus had all the qualities men idolize. He was a carpenter's son. He came from the peasantry. He rose up from the masses, as have many popular leaders before and after Him. He did not lack leadership. At His command strong men left their successful businesses to follow Him. He even had organizational abilities. He delegated responsibility to His disciples, divided His followers into two-man evangelistic teams, and when the crowds before Him were hungry, He

139

divided them into groups of fifty and saw that every person was fed.

He was brave. He faced a wild man possessed with two thousand devils. When Herod vowed to capture Him, He called the king a fox and vowed to go right on with His ministry. He had no fear. He was a just Man, the Man of the ages. It seemed that He was the perfect Man to lead the greatest popular movement of all time. Instead He was rejected, denounced, rebuffed, refused, repressed, restrained, reproached, and repudiated. Why?

He was rejected because, instead of choosing the path to popular leadership, Jesus chose the road to Calvary. He did not want the approval of the masses. He chose instead to offer those same masses salvation. He chose the cross over the glamour of popular acclaim. He chose to give His own body and blood for the salvation of the human race.

Since that time Calvary has borne an ugly stigma. It is popular to wear a cross around one's neck or to use a cross to decorate a church. These crosses remind us of the work of Christ. It is a beautiful symbol. Still there is a stigma to the cross. Jesus said, "If any man will come after me, let him deny himself, and take up his cross, and follow me. For whosoever will save his life shall lose it: and whosoever will lose his life for my sake shall find it" (Matt. 16:24,25). We have already spoken of the three steps to discipleship. And we have already learned that the term "taking up one's cross," as used here, speaks of death. In the days of Roman crucifixion, one did not pick up a cross to march in a parade. One picked up a cross only to bear it to his place of execution.

Jesus has borne His cross and borne it well. His work is completed. He does not ask us to pick up His cross. He asks us to pick up *ours*. That is why the cross still bears such stigma. We, as believers, must take up our own crosses in order to follow Christ. Taking up that cross may not be pleasant or easy, but it is necessary.

THE CROSS: A PLACE OF SEPARATION

The first reason for the stigma of the cross is the separation it represents. When we take up our cross to follow Christ we are separated from everything. The cross separated Jesus from His family and friends. He hung on the cross; they didn't. The cross we bear will have the same effect. If we follow Christ and place our lives totally at His disposal, we may be separated from our family and friends. We may be separated from our ideals. We may be separated from our most prized possessions. The cross is a place of separation. This separation, however, has a positive aspect as well. Not only may we face separation from the things we have held dear, but we may also experience a divine separation from the power of sin.

The Lord Jesus Christ, in dying for us, bore all of our sins in His body. Even more, He took upon Himself our inherited sinful nature. That thing which we inherited from Adam, that thing which seems to drive us to sin, was nailed with Christ to the cross. When we follow Jesus to the cross, the stranglehold that sins once held on our lives is broken. Just as our acceptance of Christ has separated us from the eternal penalty of sin, so our willingness to take up our cross with Jesus separates us from the power of sin. Calvary is a place of separation.

THE CROSS: A PLACE OF DESERTION

Calvary is also a place of desertion. When Jesus was handing out food, healing sick people, and raising the dead, masses thronged about Him. By the time He reached Calvary, most of them had deserted Him. At Calvary His enemies far outnumbered His friends. Even the disciples who had walked with Him so closely fled in fear. Those who would truly be Christ's disciples should expect desertion. Those who do not understand the message of Christ, and those who understand the message but reject it, will desert the one who goes to the cross with our Lord.

THE CROSS: A PLACE OF MISUNDERSTANDING

Calvary is also a place of misunderstanding. Many people avoid it for this reason. Jesus' own mother could not understand the cross. She stood weeping. Peter did not understand it. He cut off the ear of one man who tried to take Jesus to the cross. Calvary is a place of misunderstanding. When we are genuinely saved and take up the cross to follow the Lord, some of our best friends will say, "I do not understand you any more." They may not understand why we no longer desire the things we once desired. They may not understand our new interest in God's Word.

Only God, and those who receive life through His

Son, can truly understand the cross. The unregenerate man, the man who has not been washed in the blood of Christ, cannot understand what the cross represents. To him it is a mystery, a place of misunderstanding.

THE CROSS: A PLACE OF RIDICULE

Calvary is also a place of ridicule. At Calvary the priests sneered at Jesus. Crowds gathered to watch Him die. They wagged their heads and mocked Him, saying, "If You could tear down the temple and raise it up again in three days, why don't You come down from the cross?" Most of us don't like ridicule. For that reason, we stay away from Calvary. We may be willing to accept the salvation Jesus gives us, but we are not willing to take up our cross and follow Him to the place of crucifixion. But Jesus could not have saved the world without Calvary. There could be no Holy Communion without Calvary. There could be no life, strength, edification, joy, nor peace without Calvary.

Likewise, we cannot be His true disciples without going to Calvary ourselves, in our own personal way. That trip to Calvary will include ridicule. Cruel soldiers cursed Jesus, and elite priests, dressed in the finest of garments, laughed at Him. Some of us could not stand that. If someone were to accuse us of being fanatics, or "holy rollers," or old-fashioned, some of us would leave the good church we attend and go hide in a church that is as cold as ice. To avoid ridicule we would run to a church that is as lifeless as a sepulchre and sit there, week after week, among the dead.

143

Ridicule is more than many believers can endure. But this is not what God wants from us. Jesus bore ridicule, and He expects us to bear our own crosses and follow Him, even if the path is one of ridicule.

THE CROSS: A PLACE OF HUMILIATION

Calvary is also a place of humiliation. There is no pride at Calvary. When Jesus came to Calvary the executioners divested Him of everything He had. They hung Him naked before the crowd and gambled for His cloak. Humiliation is a part of bearing the cross. Before we can be truly effective for Christ, before we can be His disciples, we must realize that there is nothing in us worthy of God's grace. We must realize that our pride is totally without basis. Sometimes we must be publicly humiliated before coming to this realization. Jesus, though He could have called on angels from heaven to hide His nakedness and rescue Him from His place of humiliation, allowed Himself to become a public spectacle. Now He calls upon us to follow Him there.

It is not so much that God wants us to be humiliated, any more than He wants us to be ridiculed or misunderstood or deserted or separated from the things we love. Nevertheless, God wants us to be as willing to bear humiliation as Christ was. Sometimes the way of the cross is a humiliating path. Sometimes our stand for God may require payment of a devastating price. But when we face such humiliation, we should realize that Christ faced it also. If the Son of God, pure and perfect, could face the humiliation of being executed with the wicked, then we, by the power of the Holy Spirit, should be able to bear the humiliation that comes into our lives.

THE CROSS: A PLACE OF SUBMISSION

Calvary, in still a greater sense, was a place of submission. One of the things we have inherited from Adam is a free will. That will is strong. We want to have our own way. We want to go where we want to go. We want to be what we want to be. We want to live the way we want to live. Calvary, on the other hand, is a place of submission. Calvary is a place where we must say, "Not my will, but Thy will be done."

Calvary is a place where we submit to the will of God. When we go to the cross, our will is no longer important. It is no longer important where we want to go. It is no longer important what we want to be. The only thing that is important is that Christ said, "Take up thy cross and follow Me." Calvary is a place where that strong will we have inherited from Adam is nailed to the cross of Roman crucifixion. If we would follow Christ we must realize that our will is now His will.

THE CROSS: A PLACE OF SACRIFICE

We may further describe Calvary as a place of sacrifice. Jesus, as the Lamb of God, was the fulfillment of all the Old Testament sacrifices. All of those sacrifices pointed forward to the time when the Son of God would offer Himself as the great and final sacrifice for the sins of mankind. It was at Calvary, upon the cross, that Jesus made the ultimate sacrifice: He gave His blood and His flesh for mankind. Following Christ, in the truest sense, involves sacrifice as well. Sacrifice is not the normal thing for human beings. Man does not want sacrifice. Man is interested in man; self is interested in self. Taking up the cross demands sacrifice. Discipleship demands sacrifice.

Such sacrifice extends beyond merely giving of one's time or energies. If we are to be Christ's disciples we must be willing to sacrifice ourselves wholly to Him. This means placing our lives at His disposal, putting all that we hold dear upon the altar and giving God permission to use all according to His will. Sacrifice means no longer thinking of ourselves first, but placing Christ first. Sacrifice is more than giving, it is giving up. Sacrifice is the surrender of our lives to God. This is basic to discipleship. Those who would take up the cross and follow Christ must be willing to sacrifice themselves completely to Him.

THE CROSS: A PLACE OF DEATH

Most of us agree that Calvary is a place of separation. It is a place of desertion, misunderstanding, ridicule, humiliation, submission, and sacrifice. Ultimately Calvary is also a place of death. It was at Calvary that Christ died. It was at Calvary that His flesh was torn and His blood was spilled. It is at Calvary that the perfect life was cut off so that the imperfect could have eternal life. For Jesus the cross meant death. For His disciples it can mean no less.

The Stigma of the Cross

As sons of Adam we are inherently evil. It is our nature. Nothing can be done to change that fact. A dog is always a dog. We may bathe him, dress him, seat him at our table, and call him a member of our family; but he is still a dog. He did nothing to become a dog. He was simply born a dog. Nothing he can do, nor anything that others might do to him, will ever make him anything but a dog. So it is with the sons of Adam. We are sinners. We did nothing to become sinners. We were born that way. We may bathe ourselves, dress ourselves in the robes of religion, seat ourselves at the table of God's blessing, and call ourselves children of God; but we are still sinners. We have been sinners from the moment we were born, and will be until the moment we die. This is precisely why the cross is a necessity.

When Jesus went to Calvary, He went there for us. He bore in His own body our sin so that we might bear His righteousness. Miraculously, mysteriously, in a way we can hardly understand, God placed all our sins upon Christ. When we accept Him by faith, all of His righteousness is imputed to us. We are placed in Christ, so that the death of Christ becomes our death. The payment that Christ made becomes our payment. We are sinners until the day we die, but according to God's reckoning we died in Christ.

We are sinners until our death, but in Christ our death has already been accomplished. Our old, Adamic nature has been crucified with Christ. What we could not do by cleansing ourselves or clothing ourselves or behaving in a certain fashion or calling ourselves by a certain name, Christ accomplished for us by dying on the cross. Calvary is a place of death. It was there that Christ died. it was there that we, who are His by faith, died as well.

THE CROSS: A FINISHED WORK

We should understand that there are two aspects to the work of the cross. First, there is the work Christ accomplished for us once and for all. Second, there is the work He still accomplishes in us. The work Christ accomplished for us on the cross is finished. Nothing more is needed to separate us from the penalty of sin. No further sacrifice is necessary. No more of Christ's precious blood need be shed. No more stripes are to be laid upon His body. The work He did for us stands on its own. When we accept Him as Savior we are saved, one hundred percent saved. Were God to require our lives of us at the moment of salvation, we would be no less saved, nor any more saved, than the saint who has served God faithfully for many years. When we accept God's offer of salvation, we get salvation.

THE CROSS: AN ONGOING WORK

Still, there is a second aspect to our salvation. It is a growing process. It is the process by which we come into an intimate and personal relationship with the Lord. The new birth is exactly that, a new birth, a new beginning. The tiny baby born into an earthly family is just as much a member of that family as the most mature adult. Still, he is just a baby. His parents are eager for him to reach maturity. They look forward to seeing the small child progressively become an adult.

So it is with God. At the moment of salvation we become as much a member of God's family as we will ever be. But God is not pleased for us to remain babes. He wants us to grow. The second aspect of the cross is concerned with this process of growth. When we were born again we were transferred from the family of Adam into the family of God. Our name was changed. Our heritage was changed. The old was put away, and the new ushered in. Unfortunately, as long as we continue to inhabit this body, this temporary tabernacle that is organically linked to Adam, We carry with us vestiges of our old life. Death, and death alone, can separate us from those reminders of our former self.

Again, the cross comes to our rescue. God does not want us to commit suicide so that we will no longer sin. He wants us to allow the cross to work in our lives, putting to death, on a daily basis, those traces of the flesh.

How does this take place? It occurs much as it occurred in the life of Jesus. All the pain and suffering that Christ endured at the cross was inflicted on Him by outside sources. In a similar fashion, God may allow outside sources to inflict temporary pain, temporary sorrow, or temporary discomfort on us in order to accomplish His goals.

He may allow difficult circumstances to enter our lives that would separate us from the people or things we hold dear. Such separation, however, has only one end. As we are separated from people and things in this world, we are drawn closer to Jesus Christ. In this way Calvary is, again, a place of separation.

From time to time the people we trust and love the most may desert us. God knows it, and we may be sure that He allows it. But He does not allow such desertion out of cruelty. He allows us to be deserted by family and friends so that we will collapse into His arms and there, resting upon His breast, realize that He will never desert us.

God may allow our motives and our actions to be misunderstood. Such an experience is often painful. The pain is driven away, however, when we recognize such misunderstanding as the work of God, the work of the cross. For when all others misunderstand us, we are driven to the One who always understands, God Himself.

Trials and tribulations may crush us. Our pride and self-respect may be dashed upon the rocks, and we may find ourselves sinking in humiliation. Christ suffered such humiliation, and we should realize that God is allowing us to experience it as a part of His maturing work. Often, in our day, much is said about self-respect and self-image. Much attention is given to pride. We often forget that these things are not fruits of the Holy Spirit. There is little about self, little about that which we have inherited from Adam, that demands respect. A self-image is precisely that, an image. It is not the real thing, for the real thing is vile and degenerate and deserving of hell. As for pride, the Bible calls it an abomination. When we cling to our pride, when we cling to our self-respect and self-image, when we endeavor to see importance in ourselves, God may allow us to suffer humiliation.

Such humiliation is designed to show us we are not the center of our world, Christ is. We have value only because God values us. We are precious to Him, true, but we are precious in *spite* of what we are, not because of it.

In similar fashion, God may place us in circumstances where submission is demanded. We may work for an unsympathetic boss or be married to an unyielding mate. God may allow us to face circumstances in which we cannot have our own way, in which we cannot exercise our own will, no matter how much we might want to. Again, such circumstances are God's teachers. He uses them to remind us that our will is part of our old way of life. When we accepted His Son, we accepted His will for our lives. God often requires sacrifice. Such sacrifice is intended for our maturity. In sacrifice we are reminded that Jesus sacrificed Himself for us.

Do you understand the importance of death? Christ's death was important, because it accomplished our salvation. If we are to be all that Christ wants us to be, we must also experience death. Christ desires an intimate and personal fellowship with all believers. That fellowship is hindered by sinful remnants of the old way. The only way to remove those remnants is through death. If we are to have the full and perfect fellowship God desires for us, then some things must die. We must come to the end of ourselves. If we are not willing to go there voluntarily, God may gently and lovingly nudge us through difficult circumstances, but He intends to bring us to that point by one means or another.

WHY GO TO CALVARY?

Death, taking up the cross, becoming a disciple, is not always easy. It may be painful or unpleasant. Why should we endure it? Why should we go to Calvary? Why should we deny ourselves and take up our crosses? We do it because on the other side of Calvary is an empty tomb. After death there is resurrection.

We have heard a great deal about Christ's suffering. We have said a great deal about it in these pages. We cannot help but wonder how many believers have in the privacy of their own hearts for a few brief moments wondered if that suffering has been overstated. After all, we might reason, He was God. He knew that in just three days He would be resurrected victoriously over all sin and death and pain and sorrow and suffering. We might, for a brief moment, even suppose that we, too, could have endured a great deal of suffering if we were guaranteed such a victorious resurrection.

Those who have ever thought such things have probably felt guilty and quickly put such thoughts out of their minds. Yet there is a great deal of truth there. Why was it that Jesus declined the opportunity to become a popular leader? He had all the qualities to become a great leader and politician, but He chose Calvary, with all its pain. Why would He be willing to make such a choice? He chose that course because He knew what the outcome would be. He knew that three days later there would be a resurrection. He knew that in a very brief time there would be something new. He knew that in a few days all power in heaven and earth would be given to Him. He knew that the keys of death and hell would be His. He knew that by giving up Himself He could secure victory for all men for all time. He endured great suffering for a brief period in order to obtain victory forever. That same opportunity is ours.

We cannot become the resurrected Lord of glory, but we can share in the victory He has secured. But before that victory can be ours, we must learn something that Jesus knew. He knew there could be no victory, there could be no resurrection, there could be no eternal life, without the Crucifixion. Likewise, there can be no victory or resurrection or life for us without the cross.

When we first come to the cross, we come as sinners. We accept Jesus as Savior and He gives us eternal life. Sadly, there are many believers whose lives show no evidence of the victory Christ has won. Rather than a parade of triumph, their lives more closely resemble a funeral procession. In many cases, a funeral procession is precisely the thing that is needed. The vestiges of the old life need to be put to death on the cross. When we allow Christ to crucify and mortify our old ways of thinking and walking and talking and acting, then we become candidates for a new way of living. When we give God permission to crucify our old self, we open up the door to a life of resurrection victory. It then becomes possible for us to praise God in times of separation and desertion and misunderstanding and ridicule and humiliation. It becomes possible for us to submit our wills to God, to sacrifice our beings to Him, and to rejoice in the death of our ambitions and dreams and plans.

We can recognize that all of this is the work of Calvary, and that it leads to resurrection and a new life of joy and bliss and eternal happiness. Just as the crucifixion of Christ was the prelude to the victory over death, so the crucifixion of our old desires is the prelude to victory over the power of sin and death.

In this light the bread and cup of Communion take on new significance. When we receive the bread we should be willing to say with Christ, "I am willing to give up myself completely, to submit to the stigma of Calvary, because I know that death to my old way of life can only mean resurrection to a new way of living."

When we receive the cup, may we say, "Just as You poured out Your life for me, so I pour out my life for You. It is of no value to me. I give it up for Your use."

11
Brokenness Is Strength

Why must there be an altar? Why must we, as believers, go to the cross? Why must we sacrifice ourselves? The prophet Isaiah wrote, ". . . the lame take the prey" (Isa. 33:23). This is not regular. It is not the expected. The lion with the broken leg does not take the prey. The leopard with a broken leg does not take the prey. The incapacitated tiger does not take the prey. It is the well and the strong who take the prey.

But in spiritual matters there is something that human nature cannot understand, that there is strength in brokenness. Christ could not save the world, except on the old rugged cross. As we gain a deeper knowledge of Christ, we discover that in weakness there is strength, in brokenness there is strength, that the lame actually do take the prey.

This concept of strength manifested through weakness is foreign to human endeavor. In the human realm the best salesman makes the sale. The early bird gets the worm. And the one who is the strongest wins in the race. The one who swims fastest wins the trophy, and the one who hits the ball hardest makes the home run. In human affairs men always look for strength. In Christ, however, brokenness is strength.

The Bible says that Moses was the meekest man on earth. This was paradox. How could a person be the personal guide and leader of at least two million human beings and yet be meek? Would not he need a whip to beat his followers? Wouldn't he need a stick to prod them? Wouldn't he have to scream and curse to make them follow? No! He was the leader of two million people in a desolate wilderness. He saw that their needs were met. Yet the Bible says he was the meekest man on the face of the earth. That is brokenness! That is strength! The Lord Jesus Christ is teaching us that in the brokenness of Calvary there is strength to save the world.

HOW CAN WE KNOW THIS?

God can take the weak things of the earth and do great things with them. We see in the Bible that Noah did not display phenomenal strengths, yet he was the one God used to preserve mankind. He depended on God. He trusted in God. Joseph, though a prisoner in jail, became the right hand of the King! In God's affairs there can come a time when weakness and brokenness become strength. The Word of God says that in Christ we are more than conquerors. How can one be *more* than a conqueror? A conqueror meets a strength supposedly equal to or greater than his own and overcomes it. He meets an adversary and subdues him. How can you become *more* than a conqueror?

We become more than conquerors when someone else wins the battle for us and allows us to possess the spoils of the victory. That is what the Lord Jesus does. He wins the battle for us. In our weakness we have strength. In our weakness we have greatness. We are in Christ Jesus. We do not have to live by the brawn of the flesh or the wisdom of the mind. We can live by a Spirit so alien, so different from this world, that in our brokenness He gives us strength.

In the twelfth chapter of John's Gospel we find the story of Mary, who anointed Jesus with a special ointment. In Matthew's Gospel we learn that the ointment was kept in an alabaster box. The only way she could release this sweet spice was to break the box. With the breaking of the box the fragrance covered the Lord Jesus Christ and the one who applied it. It also covered all those who came near Him. The fragrance spread throughout the room but only because the box had been broken. As long as the ointment was in the box there was little fragrance. Only through the brokenness of the box could fragrance pour forth.

When my wife and I went to the Philippines, we had no real support of any kind except that which came from God. In six months we had only five or six people who worshiped with us. We seemed to have failed. Our hearts were broken. Then, through a great miracle wrought by God, a little girl in Bilibid prison was suddenly healed. The newspapers carried the story, with our picture, on their front pages. Overnight we had a national image, and God saved thousands and thousands of people through our ministry. Out of weakness came strength. I had no pulpit from which to preach. We met in a small rented hall. We were insignificant, but in His great strength and power He produced tremendous, glorious, amazing life.

Even though you feel insignificant, broken with disease, broken with sin, God can do for you what no one else in the universe can do. Out of brokenness He can bring fragrance, life, and blessing.

PHYSICAL WEAKNESS, SPIRITUAL STRENGTH

We can take this principle a step further by saying that the more broken we are, the more sensitive we are to God and His Spirit. This breaking process might hurt some of us. You say, "I have already been crushed." Yet if we are crushed again, we become more sensitive to the Spirit of God. We come to rely more on His strength, power, and anointing.

Learning to rely on God is what fasting is all about. We may wonder why a person should fast. In fasting we weaken the natural man, and in praying we strengthen the spiritual man. Where we have natural strength in our muscles and body, through fasting and denying our flesh strength or food we weaken that natural energy while strengthening our spiritual man through prayer and reading the Word. When our spiritual man is stronger than our natural man we can do things for God we could never do before.

That is the reason Moses fasted forty days. Elijah fasted forty days. Jesus fasted forty days. They made the natural man subside in brokenness so that the spiritual man might stand up great in strength. God can do the same for us. He can bring great strength to us through brokenness. I have known this from experience throughout the years. When we save ourselves and become strong in ourselves and sufficient in ourselves, we become spiritually impotent, useless, and helpless. If we wish God to do great things in our lives, we must realize that brokenness is strength.

This realization is central to Holy Communion. Christ was broken for us that in His brokenness we might have strength. The strength we need is in the brokenness of Christ. His body was broken so that we might have healing. And in our brokenness we will have strength. That man who is unbroken, that woman who is unbroken, is not strong in God. That strength comes only as we realize Christ dwells within us. All that we are, we are in Him. We have the strength that God wants us to have. So when we save ourselves by ourselves, we are living for ourselves instead of for God. When we are living by our own strength, we are not much use to God. But when we cannot save ourselves, then Christ is able to do something through us.

When we preserve ourselves, which most of us do, when we save our strength, when we don't give God our fullest measure of strength, when we protect ourselves and conserve our strength, we deprive ourselves of spiritual strength and power. We deny the principle that the lame take the prey. When we preserve ourselves selfishly, we lose ourselves because we are not spiritually strong.

159

When I was dying of tuberculosis and the doctors unsuccessfully tried everything they could for me, Jesus came and gave me strength. I have had it ever since. In brokenness there was strength. It was God-given, preserved at this moment by God, divine strength to carry on His service. We can all have the same strength through brokenness. Do not make excuses to God. Do not tell God that you cannot do things because of circumstances. Tell God that you are always ready to be anything, go anywhere that He directs. Trust His strength, not yours.

It was in weakness that Jacob became Israel in the Old Testament. He wrestled with the angel because he was sick and tired of himself. On one side, rushing toward him was his uncle and his army, hating him. On the other side was his brother, seeking revenge. Jacob was between a rock and a hard place. He could go no further. His strength failed. He became weak. He wrestled with that angel until the angel touched him and put his thigh out of place. He had to limp back to his family. But in that weakness he became Israel, a prince with God. When he met his brother, he was overflowing with such love that Esau's heart melted and his anger left him. Jacob was a broken man. He was no longer arrogant. He was no longer the supplanter. In brokenness, Jacob found strength.

Is it possible for God to teach us this? Must we go through life trusting in our own natural strength? Are we going to humble ourselves and say, "Lord, I can't make it alone. I can't do it by myself, but I depend upon You." In that kind of brokenness there is strength, God's strength, divine strength. Jacob discovered this and lived with it the rest of his days. We can also. We are the greatest hindrance to our own spiritual power, spiritual strength, and spiritual growth. When we are not broken we become like Lucifer. Seven times he said, "I will exalt myself to be equal to the Most High." God would not tolerate such pride in Lucifer. He will not tolerate it in us.

The greatest hindrance to spiritual power is that we are not broken. Our own natural strength cannot save us; only God can. He is our Savior, our Strength. If we insist on living by our own might, He will often allow us to do so. In fact, He may allow us to fail until that failure breaks us.

In spiritual blessing and spiritual power, we can only be useful through brokenness. Our usefulness to God and our fellowman is directly related to our brokenness. Jesus said, in John 12:24, "Verily, verily, I say unto you, Except a corn of wheat fall into the ground and die, it abideth alone: but if it die, it bringeth forth much fruit." Here is our picture of weakness becoming strength. When we place the grain of wheat in the ground, it dies. But in that death it multiplies. In that death it becomes great. In that death it becomes a supplier of human need. In brokenness it becomes strong. And in brokenness we can become a supplier of human need.

We can only be useful for the Master, and to the multitudes of the world, if we come to a place of brokenness before God. Are you willing to be broken? If you are, God will bless you. Many of us fight and resist brokenness all our lives. But God will not overlook a contrite and broken spirit. They who are broken before the Lord take the prey. They get the good things, they get the great things of life because they are moving in a different way—spiritually, not naturally or carnally.

12
The Sacrifice Bound to the Altar

We have said much of how Holy Communion reminds us of Calvary. We have also noted that the Lord's Supper reminds us of the believer's need to place himself and his life on the cross. This is a widely misunderstood subject, yet essential to victorious Christian living.

Bible students are well aware that the cross is to the New Testament message what the altar of sacrifice was to the Old Testament believer. The altar pictures the cross as surely as the sacrificial animal pictures Christ. We can learn a great deal about the relationship of the cross to our own lives by studying the altar of the Old Testament. In Psalm 118:27 we read, "God is the LORD, which hath shewed us light: bind the sacrifice with cords, even unto the horns of the altar." This Old Testament altar was approximately ten feet five inches on each side, and stood approximately six feet and three inches tall. On each of the four corners was a horn, similar to an animal horn, curving upward.

Psalm 118 is a Messianic Psalm; it speaks prophetically of the Lord Jesus Christ. This same passage, which calls for the binding of the sacrifice to the horn of the altar, also describes Jesus in verse 22, saying, "The stone which the builders refused is become the head stone of the corner." In verse 23 we read, "This is the LORD's doing; it is marvellous in our eyes." We have the Lord Jesus presented as the Central Stone, the Headstone of the divine building. Yet He was refused. We have already said that Jesus could have been a great popular leader. He did not become that leader because He chose to die for us. Because of the message He brought and the mission He carried out, the political and religious leaders of the day refused Him.

In a marvelously prophetic way, verse 26 speaks of the triumphant entry of our Lord into Jerusalem. "Blessed be he that cometh in the name of the LORD . . ." This chapter presents Jesus as the Headstone that was refused, and speaks of His triumphant entry. Almost unexpectedly, the subject changes to sacrifice. We are told to bind the sacrifice to the horns of the altar with cords. This speaks of the great altar of burnt offerings that was just inside the doors of the temple in Jerusalem. It was made of hard acacia wood and overlaid with brass. It was the center of the religion of the people. It was their altar of sacrifice, where the animals were offered before the Lord. Sacrificial animals were brought to this great altar and were bound or tied to the horns of the altar to keep them from escaping.

God was very particular about this altar. No one but a priest was allowed to minister there, and he could only do so when wearing priestly garments. One could not minister at the altar if he harbored unrepented sin in his heart, for doing so was an invitation to God to strike them dead. This altar was anointed by God, set aside for a purpose. Its horns pointed upward, speaking of divine strength, and it faced in all directions, indicating the universality of the sacrifices offered there.

The altar was also a place of safety. An individual who feared for his life could enter the temple gate and cling to the horns of the altar, the same horns to which the sacrifice was bound. As long as that person held to those horns, by law no one was allowed to harm him. This was a picture of the safety and protection of the gospel. Throughout the Old Testament the events that surrounded this altar point forward to the cross. It should not seem unusual that in the conclusion of Psalm 118 we find an invitation to bind the sacrifice to the altar. The cross is the New Testament counterpart of the altar, and Jesus is the New Testament counterpart of the sacrifice. He was rejected by the religious and political leaders of His day and bound and slaughtered as the great sacrificial Lamb.

ABRAHAM'S ALTAR

There is another instance in the Old Testament in which we find a sacrifice bound to the altar. Even before the temple was built, Abraham bound a sacrifice to an altar built of stone. That altar was the forerunner of the great altar, which was the forerunner of the cross. If the great altar speaks of the cross, then the altar of Abraham speaks of it as well. We recall the story of God's mysterious command to Abraham to sacrifice his son Isaac. Abraham did not question God's instruction. Instead he took his son and went to the place God had instructed. As the time of sacrifice approached, Isaac asked his father, ". . . where is the lamb for a burnt offering?" (Gen. 22:7). Abraham answered, ". . . My son, God will provide Himself a lamb for a burnt offering" (22:8). The two continued until they reached the top of Mount Moriah. There Abraham bound Isaac and laid him on the altar. Just when it seemed Isaac was doomed, God intervened. He stopped Abraham from sacrificing the boy and provided a sacrificial lamb to take his place.

This account brims with symbols and pictures of New Testament truth, all of which relate to the cross and to our personal experience on the cross.

First, and most obvious, is the manner in which Abraham willingly offered his son. This pictures the totally unselfish way in which God has given His Son for us. This story tells us to consider that God loved us so much that He was willing to give His Son on our behalf.

The second picture speaks of Christ as the Sacrifice. At the very moment when it seemed that Isaac was doomed, God provided a sacrifice. The sacrifice became a substitute for the one who was designated to die. So it is with Christ. We have been designated to die as the descendants of Adam. We, by our inherited natures, are sinners. The wage of our sin is death. We are doomed. Yet when it appears that we are without hope, God's sacrificial Lamb comes to our aid. Just as the ram caught in the thicket became a substitute for

Isaac, so Jesus Christ becomes a Substitute for all who will accept Him by faith.

The third picture is the one with which I am most concerned here. Though its magnitude may be beyond our comprehension, God's love is at least familiar to us. Though we may not understand Christ's willingness to die for us, we are familiar with the fact that He has become our Sacrifice. Many of us, however, have not given our full attention to those things symbolized by the bound sacrifice.

We have seen that being a true disciple of Christ requires our taking up our own crosses and following Him. We must be willing to let our hopes and dreams, our lives, be taken to the cross and sacrificed there. Remember that the Old Testament altars point to the New Testament cross. The story of Abraham and Isaac is closely related to the cross. It is also closely related to our own crosses, the crosses Christ commands us to take up. When we understand these things, the sacrifice of Isaac takes on a new dimension.

Notice the submissive attitude of Abraham. God had given him a son, an heir through whom he was to realize eternal promises. Then God commanded him to sacrifice that son on an altar. God was not commanding Abraham to give up some sin or excess. It was not an evil thing that was to be placed on the altar, it was the dearest and most precious thing that Abraham knew. All of God's promises were linked to Isaac. If Isaac died, the promises died. Isaac represented Abraham's purpose for living. Still, God demanded that Isaac be sacrificed. So Abraham obeyed.

167

Many of us live with the mistaken idea that if a thing is good or decent or wholesome, God will not require us to lay it aside. Nothing could be further from the truth. Often we settle for that which is good, when God would rather give us that which is best. In order for us to truly be disciples we must be willing to lay aside the most prized possessions of our heart. We must be willing to place everything we have upon the altar. We must be willing to give up even those things that are very good. When God calls for sacrifice on our part, He does not ask that we inconvenience ourselves. He does not ask that we go slightly out of our way to serve Him. When God calls for sacrifice, He wants sacrifice. He does not want part of us, not even the best part of us. He wants *all*. God told Abraham to place Isaac totally at His disposal. Likewise, He wants us to place all that we have at His disposal.

Notice also the willing spirit of Isaac. The Bible does not tell us that Isaac wanted to die, but it does say that he was willing to. He did not struggle, or question his father's instructions. He simply obeyed. He allowed himself to be bound and placed upon the altar, fully believing that he would shortly be put to death. This is the attitude of discipleship. This is the attitude we must possess if we are to be true disciples of Christ.

Like Abraham, we must be willing to place our most prized possessions upon the altar. We must also be willing to go there ourselves. This pictures the cross as surely as anything in the Old Testament. In Romans 12:1 Paul wrote, "I beseech you therefore, brethren, by the mercies of God, that ye present your bodies a living sacrifice, holy, acceptable unto God, which is your reasonable service." God asks for us to sacrifice ourselves. When Isaac went to the altar, he went there bound. The Old Testament animals were bound to the altar. They had come to that altar to die. There was no turning back. It was not important whether those animals were in the mood to die. No one asked them if they felt like dying. They came to die. Their will in the matter was of no consequence. When we present ourselves to God as living sacrifices, we forfeit our wills to His will. He knows best. If He chooses to lead us through difficulty and pain, we go. If He chooses to bless us with ease and plenty, we go. If He chooses to bind us, we submit. If He chooses to sacrifice us, we allow it.

This is the attitude God expects of disciples, yet it is an attitude seldom seen in Christians.

THE MEANING OF *SACRAMENT*

Yet, if we are to be His disciples we must give up ourselves entirely, as Isaac did. This brings us to consider the word *sacrament*. We have identified the memorial feast that Jesus initiated as the Lord's Supper, Holy Communion, or the Lord's Table. We have purposely avoided using the word *sacrament*, because it is sometimes misunderstood. Some believe that we receive salvation by receiving the Lord's Supper. They refer to the Lord's Supper as a sacrament and teach that we are saved by receiving this sacrament. This is not New Testament doctrine. We are saved by receiving the Lord Jesus Christ. No one who has not received Christ can receive the Lord's Supper. We do not receive the Lord's Supper to become saved, we receive it *because* we are saved.

Still, we do not need to fear the word *sacrament*. The term originates in a word that describes the pledge taken by soldiers enlisting in the imperial army of Rome. These soldiers took an oath of absolute devotion to the emperor. They called that oath a sacrament. Since the Romans regarded the emperor as deity, their pledge to him was regarded as holy. The sacrament was a holy pledge of endless devotion to the emperor of Rome. For this reason, we can use the word *sacrament* to describe the Lord's Supper, as long as we understand what the word means.

Early Christians accepted the Lord's Supper as an oath bought by the blood of Christ. It was a promise of everlasting devotion. Jesus gave Himself for us. He allowed His body to be broken and His blood to be spilled. He became our Sacrifice. Because of that sacrifice, we have eternal life. We have hope that we could never possess without Him and strength that goes beyond ourselves. Because of what He has done for us, God calls on us to enter into a sacrament, a holy pledge of our devotion to Christ. We are to become living sacrifices to Him. We are to give up the things we desire most if He requires them. We are to place ourselves at His disposal. We are to surrender our wills to His will. We are to allow ourselves to be bound and sacrificed on His altar. The symbol of this oath, this pledge of devotion, is the Lord's Supper. The broken bread and the cup remind us of what

Christ has done for us. They remind us of the reason we are willing to present ourselves to Him.

THE LAMB OF GOD

In the New Testament the Lord Jesus gave Himself at Calvary. When His disciples begged Him not to go to Jerusalem, He did not yield to their pleading. His heart was set on going to Jerusalem so that He could present Himself as a Sacrifice. He had the same attitude as Abraham and Isaac. He was willing to give up Himself, and all that He had, for others.

How beautifully the Old Testament has presented to us the truth of the New Testament. Many of us have never realized the deeper significance of the bread and the cup of Holy Communion. They mean simply that God has an altar. God has never changed His way of salvation. God had an altar in the Old Testament. That was where the people came to receive their forgiveness of sin. There was blood on that altar. Christ could not save you and me without blood. Without blood, without sacrifice, there could be no salvation.

The bread and the cup tell us that God has an altar and that Jesus Christ went to that altar for us. His body was broken for us, His blood shed for us.

The Lord's Supper also teaches that God has an altar for us. When we receive the broken bread, the picture of Christ's body, we are reminded that God wants us to sacrifice ourselves as fully for Him as Jesus did for us. When we receive the cup, we are reminded that God expects us to pour ourselves out as completely as Jesus did. The Lord's Supper teaches us that the cross, the altar, is more than a religious symbol. It is more than a means of execution. The altar, the cross, must symbolize our attitude of total sacrifice and submission to God.

When we receive the Lord's Supper, may it be a reminder of all that Christ has given for us and a challenge to give our all for Him.

13
Memorials

When we think of Holy Communion, the word that comes immediately to mind is *memorial*. The word *memorial* comes from the same root as the word *memory*. Memorial gardens are places of memory. They are places where we plant the earthly remains of our loved ones and where we can go to remember those loved ones. Memorials are aids to the memory. God has given various memorials, knowing that remembering certain people or events will aid our spiritual wellbeing.

We read in John 6:48 the Words of Jesus, "I am that bread of life." In verses 56–58 He said,

> He that eateth my flesh, and drinketh my blood, dwelleth in me, and I in him. As the living Father hath sent me, and I live by the Father: so he that eateth me, even he shall live by me. This is that bread which came down from heaven: not as your fathers did eat manna, and are dead: he that eateth of this bread shall live for ever.

These Words of Jesus are revolutionary. The people who heard Him were shocked. He was offering them something that had come straight from heaven, something brand new. He was showing them that there were some important memorials for them to observe. When He led His disciples into the upper room He said, ". . . this do in remembrance of me" (Luke 22:19). When Jesus died, there was no funeral. After His resurrection, there was no need for a gravestone. There was no memorial service and there is no memorial. The only physical link we have with our resurrected Savior is the Communion Supper He left for us. When we share that Supper we have communion and remember the life He lived, the death he died, and the resurrection He has achieved. This memorial of the church must remind us that God has always had memorials. The memorial He gave in the Last Supper is only one of many in Scripture.

OLD TESTAMENT MEMORIALS

In the beginning pages of Scripture we find Abel, who built an altar and offered a lamb unto God. Why would he do such a thing? That sacrifice was a memorial to the fact that his father had fallen into sin in the Garden, and to the grace of God who, through the death of an animal, clothed Adam and Eve. Abel's altar was a memorial altar. Memorials are not something new with God.

A little further forward in history we come to Noah. We are all familiar with the devastating flood that God sent in Noah's day. Each man, woman, boy, and girl, with the exception of Noah and his family, was destroyed. All animal life, except that which was preserved in the ark, was also destroyed. After the flood had ended, God established a memorial. He designated the rainbow as an eternal symbol of that event.

Years later God chose Abraham to be the man through whom the Savior would come. He set Abraham aside. He designated him, and all of his offspring, as special. In connection with that selection, God established another memorial, circumcision. God commanded Abraham to be circumcised and to see that all of his offspring would forever observe the rite of circumcision.

Circumcision, as we discover in Philippians 3, pictures the cutting away or putting away of the old way of life. By establishing circumcision as a continual practice of the descendants of Abraham, God was establishing a permanent memorial to the selection of Abraham as distinct from the pagan and heathen people who surrounded him. Circumcision was a memorial to the fact that Abraham and his descendants were separated unto God.

As we move forward through God's Word we find a man called Jacob. Jacob was in trouble with his father. He was in trouble with his brother. Because of that trouble he ran to a place today called Bethel. He had come all the way from Hebron, a distance of some forty miles. It was a long trip, but Jacob feared for his life and wanted to get as far from home as possible. Tired from the journey, he laid down to sleep. God gave Jacob a vision. He saw angels walking up and down a staircase or ladder. When Jacob awoke he realized that God was in that place. He made a covenant with God, and as a memorial to that covenant he erected a stone altar.

Years later, when Jacob's life of deceit had gotten

him into more trouble, God called Jacob back to Bethel. Bethel was the location of the memorial, and it represented the commitment between God and Jacob. God knew that Jacob could not return to Bethel without remembering the events that had taken place there. God knew that Jacob could not return to Bethel without remembering the promise he had made God and the promise God had made him. Bethel was a memorial. Bethel still stands, a memorial to a man who met God there and did not want to forget the meeting.

Some four hundred years after Jacob built his altar at Bethel, God prepared to bring His chosen people out of the land of Egypt. During their time in that land they had gone from being guests of Pharaoh to slaves. The night that He brought them out He established a memorial with them, the Passover Feast. Every Hebrew family was instructed in the proper manner to execute this special memorial. For every home a lamb was to be killed, and the blood of that lamb was to be spread on the posts of the door. As a final judgment on the nation of Egypt, God sent His angel through the land. In every home where the blood was not applied, the firstborn died.

The Egyptians were so terrified by this display of divine power that they forced the Hebrews out of the land. But the Passover did not end with the successful escape from Egypt. God commanded the children of Israel to observe the Passover each year. In succeeding generations, when Jewish children asked the meaning of the Passover, their parents told them of the time when God delivered Israel from oppression. The

Passover was a perpetual memorial to the power of God. The Passover, celebrated each year, was a time of memory.

After being delivered from Egypt, Israel moved into the wilderness, where God gave them the law. He gave them a system of worship. He gave them a tabernacle. Things began to get better for the Hebrews. They had been slaves, but were now a nation. The men formed an army. The women began to take care of their own homes instead of the homes of their Egyptian masters. God was meeting their needs on a daily basis. They received their food directly from heaven. Aaron's rod, which had been a dead stick, budded and blossomed to reveal the presence of God with His people. When they had made the ark of the covenant to set inside the tabernacle, a sample of the bread from heaven and Aaron's rod were placed inside the ark. Also included in the ark was the brass serpent which Moses had formed, to which people had looked for healing.

These items were included in the golden box as memorials. Inside the chest was manna, which spoke of God's provision from heaven. There was a rod, symbolic of God's divine leadership. There was the brass serpent, which spoke of God's power to heal. These memorials spoke to the children of Israel constantly, reminding them that God was their Source, their Leader, and their Protector. Many good things had happened to the Hebrews. It would have been easy for them to become proud. It would have been easy for them to boast of the great things they had experienced. It would have been easy for them to forget that God had brought them every step of the way. The ark of the covenant became a box of memories, memories of the power of God and His blessings on Israel.

When the children of Israel were ready to go into the promised land, God opened up the Jordan River so they could walk on dry land. Just as He had parted the Red Sea at the beginning of their journey, He parted the waters of the Jordan River at its end. He brought them out of Egypt and into Palestine. To be certain that they did not forget the miraculous way in which He had brought them through the Jordan, God instructed the priests to remove twelve stones from the dry bed of the Jordan. Those stones were to be stacked in a pile on the river bank. For generations to come, when the young children would ask the meaning of those stones, they would be told how God opened up the river and brought the whole nation through on dry land.

He had held back the waters and they had walked through. There had been no bridges. There had been no boats. They had walked through the River Jordan. It was a miracle from God, and God established a memorial so that Israel would never forget it. Memorials are a necessity. People tend to forget the good things God has done. Memorials are teachers, constantly instructing us in the great truths of previous days.

NEW TESTAMENT MEMORIALS

The New Testament age is not without its own

memorials. God teaches His church through memorials in the same way He taught the nation of Israel. We have two sets of memorials. The first is water baptism. It is a memorial to our salvation. It reminds us that we were once sinners. It reminds us that when we accept Christ, we are with Him. It reminds us that our Adamic nature has been put away. It reminds us that, through the resurrection of Christ, we have new life. When we see water baptism we remember that we have died in Christ. When we see a new believer emerging from the baptismal waters we remember that God has raised us from spiritual death to a new life in Christ Jesus. Water baptism is a living memorial to our death, burial, and resurrection in Christ.

The other memorial God has given us is Holy Communion, the Lord's Supper. Jesus knew that when He returned to heaven men would forget all that He had done. He determined to establish a memorial to the work He had accomplished, one that would always be fresh in the minds and hearts of mankind. He established a memorial that would continually point back to His work on the cross, and forward to His return.

Incorporated in that memorial are two emblems. The bread reminds us of His broken body. The cup reminds us of His shed blood. We are reminded that through His broken body we can have healing, and through His blood, salvation. In that memorial supper we can remember other things as well. We are reminded of our union with Christ and of the fellowship we can enjoy with other believers. We are reminded that we have been crucified to the world, and the world crucified to us. We recall the sins that killed Jesus, and we are given opportunity to examine our own lives for the presence of those sins.

The Lord's Supper makes us aware that the only way in which we can be disciples of Jesus Christ is to die ourselves, take up our crosses, and follow Him. As we recall the seven significant statements Christ uttered in His final hours upon the cross, we are reminded of the wounds He suffered and the agony all three Persons of the Godhead experienced at Calvary.

As we think of Calvary, we are reminded of the great altars of the Old Testaments and the sacrifices bound upon those altars. We realize anew that even as Christ was broken, so must we be broken if we are to have spiritual strength.

The Lord's Supper is God's great memorial. It reminds us of all that He has done for us and of all that we are because of Him. It reminds us of that which we have in common as believers and of what we can and should do to bring others to Jesus Christ. When we receive the Lord's Supper we may experience joy at His offering for us, sorrow at the pain He experienced, compassion for those who do not know Christ, gratitude for the opportunity of salvation, and many other feelings.

But above all, when we receive the Lord's Supper, we *remember*. We remember Jesus and what He did for us. We remember what He has made available to us. And we remember what He asks of us.

MY CHALLENGE TO YOU

If Jesus should come today, would you be ready? If you are not sure, I invite you to receive Jesus as your Savior now. You will be filled with hope and peace that only Jesus can offer.

Pray this prayer out loud with me right now:

"Dear Lord Jesus, I am a sinner. I do believe that you died and rose from the dead to save me from my sins. I want to be with you in heaven forever. God, forgive me of all my sins that I have committed against you. I here and now open my heart to you and ask you to come into my heart and life and be my personal Savior. Amen."

When you pray the Sinner's Prayer and mean it, He will come in instantly. You are now a child of God and you have been transferred from the devil's dominion to the kingdom of God.

Read I John 1:9 and Colossians 1:13. A wonderful peace and joy will fill your soul.

Please write and tell me what Jesus has done for you. I will send you a little pamphlet titled, "So You're Born Again!"

Mail your letter to:
Lester Sumrall
P.O. Box 12, South Bend, IN 46624

You can help Lester Sumrall
WIN A MILLION

God has called Lester Sumrall to win a million souls to Christ through the outreaches of the LeSEA ministry Lester Sumrall Evangelistic Association. He showed him that the only way this would be possible is for friends and partners to work with him, pooling their resources to get the gospel out in every way possible.

When you join Brother Sumrall in this effort, you become a member of the Win-A-Million Club. Each month, you send your faithful gift of $20 or more to help with our soul winning outreaches. . .

Christian television channels:
WHME-South Bend, WHMB-Indianapolis, KWHB-Tulsa, KWHE-Honolulu, WHKE-Kenosha/Chicago
WHME-FM Christian radio and WHRI shortwave radio.
World Harvest Homes
Missionary assistance
Feed The Hungry, International
World Harvest Magazine
World Harvest Bible College, South Bend
Christian Center School
Satellite T.V.
Video Teaching Tape Ministry
Books, tracts, pamphlets, teaching syllabi
Campmeetings—Conferences—Crusades
Christian Center Cathedral of Praise

As a Win-A-Million partner, you receive a beautiful gold lapel pin and the World Harvest Magazine. Simply write to Dr. Lester Sumrall at P.O. Box 12, South Bend, Indiana 46624, and say, "Here's my gift to help. I want to be a Win-A-Million partner."

Approved for Veteran Training
A.A. and B.A. Degrees

Running with the vision of winning a million souls to Christ. Dr. Lester Sumrall Founder & President

A SCHOOL WITH A VISION

V ery highest academic standards

I nvestment return; Top-quality education at bottom-dollar tuition

S piritual emphasis - Full Gospel

I nteraction - highly personalized faculty-student relationship

O n the job training while in school

N ationally and internationally known guest teachers

Write: WHBC, P.O. Box 12, South Bend, IN 46624

World Harvest Magazine is Dr. Sumrall's pulpit to the world. This bi-monthly magazine contains sermons, a question & answer page where he answers questions asked by the readers and news about what is happening at LeSEA.

For your free copy, write

World Harvest Magazine, P.O. Box 12, South Bend, Indiana, and ask to be added to the mailing list.

Imagination, Hidden Force of
Human Potential

Imagination gives birth to empires, fortunes, art, music, literature, architecture, and new inventions. Imagination is a tremendous force—it is creative in becoming the person Christ wants you to be.

How To Know
THE WILL OF GOD

How can I find God's will for my life?
You can know God's will by listening to His voice. Walk in His Word as He has identified it to you. Then when God says do something, just do it!

Conscience, The
Eternal Scales of Justice

Your conscience is a watchman over your soul. This generation has a conscience burned out as by a hot iron, and many people do not know right from wrong.

Each book: REG. $1.95   **NOW $1.49**

. . . . .CLIP COUPON AND RETURN TO LeSEA. . . . .

P.O. Box 12, South Bend, IN 46624

_____IMAGINATION   #31061 . . . . $ _____

_____CONSCIENCE   #31085 . . . . $ _____

_____HOW TO KNOW THE WILL OF GOD
              #31045. . . . . $ _____

TOTAL AMOUNT OF ABOVE ITEMS. . . .$ _____

To be paid in U.S. currency; Canadian orders add 35% $ _____

Add 50¢ per book for postage and handling. . . .$ _____

TOTAL PURCHASES. . . .$ _____

NAME _____

ADDRESS _____ PHONE NO. (_____)_____

CITY _____ STATE _____ ZIP _____

☐VISA Exp. Date _____ ☐MASTERCARD Exp. Date _____

SIGNATURE _____

185

Living Happy Ever After

The highest tower of global strength, the very cement that holds the collective body of Homo sapiens in the unity of the society of men, is the home. It is the truth...There is no place like home.
Lesson titles:

● *The Birth Of The Human Family* ● *What Is Family Life?* ● *The Three Worlds Of Marriage* ● *The Right Relationship Between Man And Woman* ● *The Unfaithful Wife* ● *The Unfaithful Father -In-Law* ● *The King's Stepdaughter* ● *Seven Woman And One Man* ● *America's 3,000 Divorce Courts* ● *Ten Family Hurdles* ● *Ten Principles Of Marital Bliss* ● *Ten Deadly Destroyers Of Living Happy Ever After* ● *Protecting Your Home*

☐ Please send me Living Happy Ever After
Syllabus & 8 tapes............................. $42.00
Please send _____ syllabus................... $ 10.00
☐ Please send tapes series....................... $32.00

ADD 7% FOR POSTAGE & HANDLING....................$ _____
INDIANA RESIDENTS ADD 5% TAX.....................$ _____

(PAY IN U.S. CURRENCY, CANADIAN   **TOTAL $**_____
ORDERS ADD 35%)

☐ VISA ☐ MASTERCARD Exp. Date _____
_____
CREDIT CARD NUMBER

_____
SIGNATURE   OF   CARDHOLDER

_____
NAME

_____
STREET   ADDRESS

_____
CITY   STATE   ZIP
Phone   (_____)_____

LeSEA, Inc., P.O. Box 12, South Bend, IN 46624

BOOKS BY DR. LESTER SUMRALL

- Adventuring With Christ
- My Story To His Glory
- Take It—It's Yours
- Gifts & Ministries Of The Holy Spirit
- Alien Entities
- Battle Of The Ages
- Conscience—The Scales Of Eternal Justice
- Demons The Answer Book
- Bitten By Devils
- Ecstasy—Finding Joy In Living
- Faith To Change The World
- Faith Under Siege; The Life of Abraham
- Fishers Of Men
- Gates Of Hell
- Genesis—Crucible Of The Universe
- Hostility
- Hypnotism—Divine Or Demonic
- Imagination—Hidden Force Of Human Potential
- I Predict 2000 A.D.
- Jerusalem, Where Empires Die—
  Will America Die At Jerusalem?
- Jihad—The Holy War
- Living Free
- Making Life Count
- Miracles Don't Just Happen
- 101 Questions & Answers On Demon Power
- Paul—Man Of The Millennia
- Run With The Vision
- Secrets Of Answered Prayer
- Sixty Things God Said About Sex
- Supernatural Principalities & Powers
- 20 Years Of ''I Predict''
- The Battle Of The Ages
- The Making Of A Champion
- The Names Of God
- The Reality Of Angels
- The Stigma Of Calvary
- The Total Man
- The Will—The Potent Force Of The Universe
- The Human Body
- The Human Soul
- The Human Spirit
- Trajectory Of Faith—Joseph
- Unprovoked Murder
- You Can Conquer GRIEF Before It Conquers You
- Miracles And The Sumrall Family
  (by Leona Sumrall Murphy)
- The Marriage Triangle (Leona Sumrall Murphy)

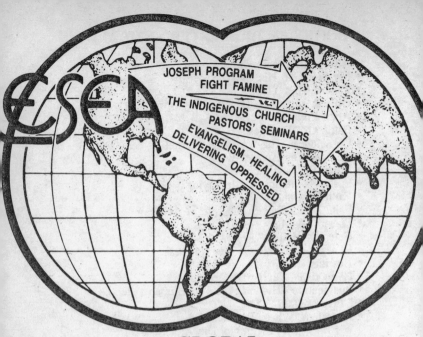

GLOBAL FEED-THE-HUNGRY PROGRAM

LeSEA is introducing a unique "Joseph Program" to help feed Christians who live in areas plagued by famine. While he was in Israel with a group of pilgrims, the Lord asked Dr. Sumrall to initiate a global program to combat hunger and he was told in detail how to tackle such a herculean task. God declared that the aggressive attack against the forces of evil should be three-pronged. How can this be done?

Seminars will be held in famine areas when the people are ministered to spiritually. We will pray for the sick and deliver those in bondage. Pastors will then be given food and other supplies which they will distribute among their own congregations. This will elevate the pastor in the eyes of their people.

We are looking for 10,000 pastors to challenge world hunger by including "Feed the Hungry" in their missionary giving. Laymen are asked to join "The King's Court" and laywomen are asked to join "The Queen's Court" to fight famine. By doing so, you will be kept informed as to what you can do. Fill out the entry blank and return to the address given. Let us hear from you today. We must act now! Tomorrow may be too late!

FEED THE HUNGRY
JOIN THE KING'S COURT!

NAME _____

ADDRESS _____

CITY _____

STATE _____ ZIP _____

THE END-TIME "JOSEPH PROGRAM" • *Untold Millions Die Of Hunger*
SOUTH BEND, IN 46680-7777, USA

· ·

FEED THE HUNGRY
JOIN THE QUEEN'S COURT!

NAME _____

ADDRESS _____

CITY _____

STATE _____ ZIP _____

THE END-TIME "JOSEPH PROGRAM" • *Untold Millions Die Of Hunger*
SOUTH BEND, IN 46680-7777, USA